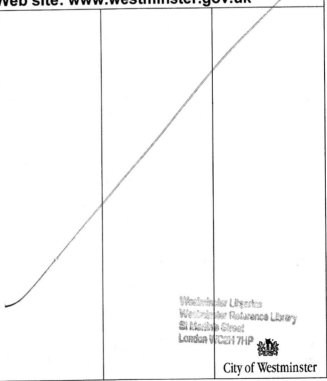

The Films of

John Garfield

by Howard Gelman

Introduction by Abraham Polonsky

The Citadel Press   Secaucus, N.J.

For
Harry Gelman,
born in the same streets, one of many.
These were his years also.

I am grateful to the Wisconsin Center for Theatre Research, for providing research material, photographs, films and facilities; to Susan Dalton, archivist at the Center, for aid in all stages of preparation of the manuscript; to Mr. Abraham Polonsky, for reading and commenting on the manuscript; to Mrs. Roberta Garfield Cohn, for granting an interview; to the *Velvet Light Trap* magazine, for printing the original articles on John Garfield; and to Melodie Knisley, Laurie Karls, Gerald Peary, and Jean Taylor, for their help.

Grateful acknowledgment is also made to the following authors and publishers, for permission to print excerpts from their books:

Harold Clurman, *Lies Like Truth*, Macmillan Publishing Co., 1956.

Paul Green, *Plough and Furrow*, Samuel French, Inc., 1963.

Charles Higham and Joel Greensberg, *The Celluloid Muse*, Henry Regnery Co., 1969.

First paperbound printing
Copyright © 1975 by Howard Gelman
All rights reserved
Published by Citadel Press
A division of Lyle Stuart, Inc.
120 Enterprise Ave., Secaucus, N. J. 07094
In Canada: George J. McLeod Limited
73 Bathurst St., Toronto, Ont.
Manufactured in the United States of America by
Halliday Lithograph Corp., West Hanover, Mass.

Library of Congress Cataloging in Publication Data

Gelman, Howard.
    The films of John Garfield.

    1. Garfield, John. I. Title.
PN2287.G377G4   791.43'028'0924   75–19080
ISBN 0-8065-0620-2

CONTENTS

Introduction by Abraham Polonsky

I met John Garfield when I went to see him and his partner, Robert Roberts, to tell them the story of *Body and Soul*. A new friend, Arnold Manoff, had just come to work at Paramount Pictures, just a few blocks away from Enterprise Studios. Manoff had been trying to make something of the Barney Ross story, but somehow he wasn't getting anywhere, and since he found me numb with Paramount, he suggested that I go over and see what I could do with some sort of prizefighter story for Garfield. But first, we had lunch at Lucey's. The match game was going on all around us, but Manoff was telling me about John Garfield and Enterprise. He made it sound like an ironic dream. It was.

Arnold Manoff is one of the best short-story writers of the depression years. That world of want, poor New York Jews, the Enlightenment, and Utopian Socialism, the Life of Reason haunting the glorious future, was the heart of *Body and Soul*. It is Romance with Rebellion. Clifford Odets, of course, was an electric part of this literary movement, and his plays were their enchanting vision, but Garfield was the star for the whole world, the romantic Rebel himself.

In a way, I found the ambiguity of the movies much like the souls of Odets and Garfield when I got there after the war. John McNulty was at Paramount when I turned up. What was I doing there? he asked me. I belonged back in New York. The race track was the only real thing around. The whole place was a fraud. He himself was just hanging in to get enough money to go back to the city, and he cursed Los Angeles, the sunlight, the palm trees, and the movies. He took me onto a set, the first I saw before the Paulette Goddard one, and he showed me Alan Ladd standing on a box for a tight two-shot in a love scene. "This is it," he said. "Go home."

He never went home, but the Blacklist sent Garfield and me back to New York.

The children of rich Jews in those days when they were attracted to the arts had a tendency to become infatuated with the avant garde and the vitality of the irrational, but most poor Jews who didn't join the money system gravitated to socialism, vague or definite; rebellion, moderate or tough; and self-consciousness, harsh or neurotic. Some became gangsters; most joined the establishment of which crime is, after all, as my friend Ira Wolfert says, "the grease that makes things run" (cf. *Force of Evil*, based on Ira Wolfert's novel *Tucker's People*).

As an actor Garfield was the darling of romantic rebels—beautiful, enthusiastic, rich with the know-how of street intelligence. He had passion and a lyrical sadness that was the essence of the role he created as it was created for him. In the hysterical tragedy in which he found himself he became an exile in his own country. That others before him and others after him in every age would play the same role was no satisfaction to him. He was ambitious. The Group trained him, the movies made him, the Blacklist killed him. The popular story, for instance, is (and he may have said so in public himself, for he was obliging in other things besides politics) that he refused the part of Kowalski in Tennessee Williams's play because the woman's part was better than the man's. I read the play when it was submitted to his company, and I know the part was turned down by Roberts because Irene Selznick wouldn't make a proper moving-picture deal on it, so Roberts decided. Garfield was unlikely to turn down anything because a part was smaller or bigger, although he liked to be the star. Everything he did flowed from his magic and frustrating years in the Group. The play was the heart of it. The ensemble was the soul of it. He knew it and acted like that on both occasions when we worked together.

Garfield felt himself inadequate as an intellectual. Most serious actors feel like this. They aren't actually inadequate, any more than intellectuals are, but they feel that way. Being an intellectual and being an artist aren't genetically paired, any more than being an artist and being a good character. Being an intellectual is a full-time occupation, and although it, like everything else, is enriched by other talents, it has its own universe and its own cast of fools. As an actor Garfield was total, and he could play an intellectual with the same vigor and astonishing rapport as a cab driver. Regarding *Force of Evil* he told me before we started that although he really didn't understand some of the meanings, the minute he hung that Phi Beta Kappa key on his watch chain he was in business. And so he was. He had the true actor's genuine wisdom for the human, and he could play his kind of intellectual just as well as he could play his kind of cab driver. You won't meet either in New York, but you wish you could.

He didn't have the range of an Olivier but then Garfield was a star who represented a social phenomenon of enormous importance for his times and, perhaps, ours too. He lived as a star without contradiction in the imagination of those who loved him for something that lay dormant in themselves, and this was tuned to the social vigor of the time that created him. Naturally, when those times became the political target of the establishment in the United States, Garfield, whose roles,

whose training, whose past were the environment of the romantic
rebellion the depression gave birth to, became a public target for the
great simplifiers. From his dead body and those of many like him,
from the hysteria and know-nothing rage of McCarthyism, HUAC,
and Nixon, there rose the ominous star of Watergate, which today
bewilders us as Nazism bewilders the German people.

Garfield knew on the night he died that Clifford Odets had that day
testified before the House Un-American Activities Committee and there,
in general, had made the popular derogatory remarks about the left
and communism. In addition, Odets said he had been a member
of the Communist party in the past.

> MR. TAVENNER: Were any of the meetings held in
> your house?
> MR. ODETS: No, I don't think I had a home then. I
> was a very poor man.

And so were the people he named. John Garfield, who wasn't even
a fellow traveler, refused to speculate, refused to name names on the
grounds he couldn't remember anyone who was a member of the
Communist party, not in the Group, not in Hollywood, not anywhere.
For years the federal government used their resources to prove he had
perjured himself, and for years they failed, but they did succeed
in killing him.

The former Mrs. Garfield says, "I believe in fate, and he might have
died anyway. But he wouldn't have died so angry. He was so angry."

He had a right to die angry. He had a right to be angry, for he could
find no way to free himself from those who were destroying him.

Now, here, on this terrible night, wandering like Joe Morse around
New York, talking to himself with a voice from the grave, really with
no place to go, rejected, he saw far off on those screens his own face,
which had become the face of a generation of New York street kids.
I joined those same New Yorkers and we stood across the street from
the funeral parlor watching the tumult and fifty policemen with white
gloves. Later, the papers said ten thousand people had come, nothing
so big since the death of Valentino.

The strangers I stood with, and they were quiet, unlike those who got
into the event, were the same I saw forming a great line around
the Globe Theatre in New York after *Body and Soul* opened, the same
faces, the same figures, the same bodies, and the same life. They
understood in terms of the romantic rebel from the streets that even
though he was torn and tempted, he could never give in.

The political vultures who flew about him and descended after his
death to croak that had he lived one more minute he, too, would have
confessed to the committee, have vanished into the ultimate irrelevance.
I hope this book reminds those who love movies of yet another star
in a world that charmed the lives of our generation, and in the end
Garfield was right to do as he did, right to act as he acted, true not
only to his generation but to the country that spawned him. Is it
important? I don't know. But it's a fact.

CALIFORNIA,
1974

At fifteen he played the part of a student in the school production of The Student Prince.

Chapter 1: Golden Boy

1952 was a year of fear. In spite of the smiling face of Dwight Eisenhower, soon to be president, in spite of a boom economy and a standard of living placing the American middle class out front in the Western world; in spite of all the earmarks of good times, fear was the undercurrent that year. We were afraid of the Russians, afraid of the nuclear doomsday, afraid of spies and saboteurs undermining our government, and even afraid of attack from outer space, from aliens! Children in schools practiced nuclear-attack drills, Americans across the country seriously built private bomb shelters.

We were obsessed by the dangers of nuclear war; perhaps because we were the only country in history that had actually used atomic weapons. We accused everyone, but mostly we pointed at each other, for 1952 was the year of the Communist confessional. We were embarked on a purge of dangerous and alien ideas; we were making the country safe, and fear was our weapon. We were fighting our first "war against Communist aggression," in Korea, but the home front was also a battlefield.

On May 20, 1952, John Garfield, Hollywood and New York actor, was found dead in the apartment of a friend in the fashionable Gramercy Park district of Manhattan—a long way from the lower East Side and the ghettos of the Bronx where he had grown up.

The last week of his life was the perfect illustration of a man living in fear. He had left his family and was living alone in a hotel; he had been smoking and drinking heavily, although he had suffered two previous heart attacks and was only thirty-nine years old. Friends described him as angry, bitter, and frustrated. What's more, he was enmeshed in a Kafkaesque situation, accused of undisclosed crimes, on the basis of undocumented evidence, trying desperately to find a way out when all doors seemed closed. He had been unofficially blacklisted from the motion-picture industry and had not worked in films for more than eighteen months. Yet he was still a popular actor. His films were still shown and watched, and his talents were sharper and more mature than ever before—he was literally at the peak of his powers.

The story of John Garfield—of his success and fall—is a view of the paradoxes and ironies inherent in the American dream. In many ways, Garfield provided proof that hard work can bring unlimited opportunity and success; and in his sudden and arbitrary fall, he provided an illustration of the precariousness of that value. One of his contemporaries has said, "More than anything else, he was a victim." A victim of what—his success? his ideals? his dreams? Hollywood? the House Un-American Activities Committee?

He was born Julius Garfinkel on New York's lower East Side on May 4, 1913. Julie was a street child from the start, like most children in the city's ghettos. They lived in overcrowded apartments, and the parents worked ten or twelve hours a day, under constant pressure for survival. So a child lived in a communal world in the open, with only his peers as authority and judge. Julie's father was a coat presser in the garment district and spent a good deal of time in the synagogue as a cantor. What little parental authority Julie had came sternly and swiftly. The family structure was a broken one for these immigrants. The father was a poor model to a son who longed to be accepted by Americans, and it was painfully obvious to the father what an inadequate figure he was for his children. On top of this, the city slums somehow undermined all the old principles of life and religion; it threw the family into contact with all kinds of people, not only the Jews of the *shtetl*. The community, while cohesive by American standards, was dispersed according to the old values. Later Julie would see his father as an "ignorant man, a religious fanatic." It was probably true and religion was also probably the father's only hold on consistency, in a life that made little sense to him outside the synagogue.

When Julie was seven, his mother died. The family had moved to the Brownsville section of Brooklyn, and his younger brother Max remained there with relatives while Julie and his father found a small apartment in the Bronx. There were more adjustments to make—this time a new mother and a father who still couldn't understand this American boy who passed for his son. The street was Julie's only freedom, and years later, Hollywood publicity departments would speak of him as having been one step away from a life of crime. More likely he would have led a life of mediocrity and frustration, as was true for so many ghetto dwellers with untapped talent. But, he attended Public School 45 in the Bronx, then under Dr. Angelo Patri, who had the revolutionary and practical idea that the city schools should train these young street urchins to do useful work.

The public-relations account of the meeting between Garfield and Patri reads like a prison movie with Pat O'Brien as the warden. "You're a sucker," Patri told him. "A sucker fights with fists; a smart boy fights with words." Even if it didn't happen that way, Julie quickly learned the right lessons. Patri's school was not a reform school or a home for boys, just a public school in the city, probably similar to today's, except that now the students are black and Puerto Rican, and their frustrations have a special edge.

This background would later make Garfield's screen

roles ring with authenticity, not because of the extreme possibilities in his life—death in the electric chair or stardom on Broadway—but because of his instinctive emotional understanding of the frustrations of the ghetto. If no one had seen his special talent, he would have been relegated to a life of obscurity and mediocrity. Luckily his talent was to be seen and heard. Putting him on the stage was the easiest way to keep him busy and away from trouble. And as soon as he was up front enjoying the spotlight, good things began to happen. He had mastered his stutter and found some proficiency as a public speaker (despite his heavy New York accent). In 1927 he won *The New York Times* citywide oratorical contest; his subject: "Franklin, the Peace Maker of the Constitution," a fitting theme for the new American boy. Patri was probably aware by now that Julie would amount to something, so Julie was given a scholarship to the Heckscher Foundation, a school where he learned the basics of theater work.

So his story was that of a bad boy who, given a chance, turned out good—a story he would portray for Hollywood many times in the next two decades. This American story says simply that if you try you will succeed; it doesn't say anything about failure or about the quality of success. The lesson Julie Garfinkel learned was simply that success was the objective, and once you had achieved it, everything was yours. He knew how to fight and how to act a little on stage, and now he was out in the world on a quest for success where street fighting helped very little and acting was hard work with small financial reward.

By 1930 he had all but become an actor—the *all but* due to the little work available and the even smaller pay. He took his turn as spear carrier and walk-on for Fritz Leber's Shakespeare players. There were odd jobs for the aspiring young actor in New York, but few paid enough to eat on, and the depression was in its volcanic stage. It seemed the wrong moment to declare yourself a man of the theater. *But at least,* the young Garfield must have mused, *if I starve as an actor, it won't be any different from starving as a desk clerk.* He landed an apprentice job with Eve Le Gallienne's Civic Repertory. Again, more spear-carrying roles, but now he had the opportunity to see the professionals work, to watch the little tricks and to practice the actor's craft.

He was a young man with a great deal of energy. That must have impressed Roberta Seidman, later Mrs. Garfield, for she remembers his first real part in a Broadway play, *Lost Boy*, starring Elisha Cook, Jr. In it he had to roar like a lion, and of course, he spent hours at the zoo watching the lions and seriously imitating their roar. But the job was small and short-lived.

At thirteen

Julie, right, in school performance of A Midsummer Night's Dream

He decided to hitchhike across the country. Many men and boys were on the road, and there was even a feeling of comradeship among the thousands who rode the freights across the United States. Later, the fan magazines would describe this trip as his odyssey through America. Everything he had done by then would be described in its most romantic vein. It wouldn't be enough for him to represent the lower class; he must embody its fantasies as well.

1932 was a big year for Jules Garfield (the name change seemed easier; it was like his own, and it was a President's as well). He traveled again across the United States, but this time on salary, with the road company of a successful New York show, *Counselor-at-law.* On the road, he acquired a new interest—he was introduced to a professor at the University of Wisconsin, Meikeljohn, who influenced him to think of returning to school. In the world of the theater, young Julie was painfully aware of his shortcomings—how little he had read, how little he knew about his country or the world. Professor Meikeljohn was well-known as an innovative teacher, and Julie was tempted. He contemplated taking examinations to return to school, but before he could give it serious thought, he received word that he was wanted for the New York company of the show. If he returned, there could be no thought of school. This was an acting part! He would speak on stage, and with him would be another man to watch and learn from—Paul Muni.

Counselor-at-law had a good run, but it did not lead to a bigger part or another show for him. Julie and Roberta took summer jobs in the Catskill Mountains to earn extra money, and this would be his steadiest source of income for the next two years.

By 1934 he was twenty-one, still hopeful, full of energy and totally dedicated to his work. He formed the most important friendships of his life at this time, with young actors like himself—dedicated, passionate, energetic, and ambitious. One friend was Clifford Odets, a Bronx neighbor and a fledgling member of a new theater group made up of young actors originally from the Theatre Guild who had set up shop under the Guild's sponsorship. Odets had told Garfield about their work, and Julie was enthusiastic, eager to become a part of it. Enthusiasm, in fact, was part of his style; he worked it and breathed it. But the new Group Theatre (as they called themselves) was not easy to get inside. Its guiding lights were Lee Strasberg, Harold Clurman, and Cheryl Crawford. They had set out to organize an idealistic ensemble company of dedicated theater people. By 1935 it was the avant-garde center of the New York theater. Among its members were Luther and Stella Adler, Franchot Tone, Morris Carnovsky, Phoebe Brand, Art Smith, Elia Kazan—the list included some of the most influential people of New York and Hollywood for the next two decades.

These were the people who formed the core of influence on the young actor—from them he got his social and political awareness, as well as his theatrical conscience, for they were dedicated to making the theater a vital and meaningful enterprise.

When they heard that Julie was wanted for a small part in the Group production of *Gold Eagle Guy*, Roberta and Julie left their summer jobs and went back to the city. There was little money in this new venture and they had to give up their summer earnings, but they came back because it was as if Julie had been called before the altar, and he could not refuse. In *The Fervent Years,* Harold Clurman noted the event: "A new apprentice was the fervid Jules Garfield."

Jules impressed everyone with his eagerness and willingness to listen, and above all, he idolized these people. There would be all-night sessions, with one or another of the directors lecturing until dawn, a few hours' sleep, and then rehearsals would begin again. Morris Carnovsky, who played father figures in so many plays, took the young actor under his wing, showed him the tricks of the trade, complimented his work, and criticized his failures.

Julie's friendship with Clifford Odets would be an important part of his professional and personal life for the next two decades. It was Odets who first noticed him in the Bronx neighborhood and first brought him into the Group, and it would be an Odets play that gave him his first big acting assignment. At that time, Odets was a hero figure for the young Garfield; he was well read, he had a passionate interest in music, and he wrote plays. Garfield's one achievement was acting; he threw all his energy into it, but he felt deficient in "cultural things." During the next several years Odets would figure prominently, either directly or indirectly, at critical points in Garfield's career; their lives would be intertwined many times for both happiness and tragedy.

So, in the company of Art Smith, Roman Bohnen, Elia Kazan, Odets, and Alan Baxter as students, and the older members of the Group, Garfield journeyed to Ellenville, New York, in the Catskills, where they all lived in an enormous house, attended classes, rehearsed, talked, and listened endlessly to lectures and discussions. He saw an intensity he had never known before, with people who, like him, were eager to work and anxious to succeed but, unlike him, had read about the world and knew about literature and art, things he was only beginning to understand. It was a magic world that summer for Jules Garfield. When the summer was

Julie, age nineteen, during the run of Counselor-at-Law, *with Katherine Locke.*

With Phoebe Brand

over, he had perfected a spectacular leap down a flight of stairs for a small part in the production of *Gold Eagle Guy.*

During the run of *Gold Eagle Guy* Odets had written and submitted to the Group his first important plays, *Waiting for Lefty* and *Awake and Sing.* Both plays were produced in 1935, and Garfield got his chance on stage as Ralph Berger in *Awake and Sing,* in which he played a young boy from a Bronx Jewish family struggling to break out of the family frustrations and constraints. It was a role written out of his and Odets's past, one he could sympathize with because he had lived it. This would be true of many of his best performances, and in a sense suited both his realistic performing style and his training in Method acting.

The Group was always in financial difficulty, and often could not find work for all its members. During lulls the actors were encouraged to take jobs in other shows if they could find them. In 1937, Odets went to Hollywood, followed by Clurman and others of the company; they discontinued rehearsals and called off the rest of the season.

Garfield took a role in the Broadway play *Having Wonderful Time,* by Arthur Kober. Billed as a "saga of the summer camps," it was a spoof on Jewish migrations to the Catskill Mountains during the summer months. Garfield played the part of a student working his way through college as a waiter; again, drawing on his experience, he did well with the part. What's more, the play was successful, and he found himself earning three hundred dollars a week, more money than he had ever seen before. "We moved out of the apartment we shared with another couple," recalled Roberta Garfield, "and for the first time we were able to help our parents, doing the kind of things young people do."

The play was a success, but Garfield still felt that real achievement could only come with the Group. Later, when Odets showed Garfield his newest play, he told his friend that the lead role, Joe Bonaparte, the Golden Boy, had been written for Garfield. There could be no doubt the part was Garfield's, not only written for him, but also sympathetically mirroring the dilemma both he and Odets would often face in the years to come. Ten years later, Odets would write *The Big Knife,* another play for Garfield that was both a mirror of their lives and a tour-de-force acting role.

Golden Boy is the story of a boxer who chooses the practical world of greed and ambition over the love of people and beauty. The lead role was Garfield's in temperament and physical build, as well as in spirit. If *Golden Boy* was the best illustration of the Odets style, it was also the quintessentially realistic role for Garfield, a role he would play with variations for years to come in the movies. Odets promised it to him, but Clurman,

Fencing with Luther Adler in the early Group days

17

the director, gave the part to Luther Adler, an established, well-known original member of the Group. Adler didn't fit the part—he was too soft and gentle-looking for the boxer—but Clurman argued that Garfield was inexperienced, not mature enough for the role.

There may have been other considerations; the production had all the earmarks of a big success for the Group, one they desperately needed. For the female lead they had brought back Frances Farmer, who was well-known through her Hollywood films. Obviously Adler was a more certain and conservative choice than the unknown Garfield. Adler would deliver a professional performance; with Garfield they would be taking a chance. But this was the one part Garfield wanted more than any other; for the first time, perhaps, he felt cheated by the Group. They had talked of experimenting, innovating, taking a chance on talent, but now, when it counted, they went to Hollywood and the established stars. He took the comic role of Siggie the cabdriver, but when the play was successful he probably felt more despondent than ever.

Garfield had been approached before by the Hollywood studios, but he hadn't given it much thought. Now, however, going to Hollywood seemed the easiest and most direct way to get back at the Group. After the first months of the *Golden Boy* run, he announced that he was leaving the show to make a film in Hollywood. The decision precipitated a crisis at the Group. Morris Carnovsky was furious; others wouldn't even speak to him. A meeting was called at which everyone vented their feelings about Garfield's decision. Clurman, unable to understand the actor's disgruntlement, blamed it on Garfield's wife.

Garfield went to Hollywood, fully expecting to return with a little more money and with his ego assuaged. He still felt himself a stage actor, and he still knew that the best acting was with the Group. His wife and child remained in New York, and he lived in a boarding house in Hollywood, because he expected his stay on the West Coast to be only temporary. Several months later, however, when *Four Daughters* was released and the reviews were in, Warner Bros. was ready to pick up the seven-year contract option on their new star.

The instant success was a little heady. Garfield had expected his scenes to wind up on the cutting-room floor, but instead, he had become a focal point of the film. This was vastly different from the stage, where you had some notion of what the final performance would look like; as a film actor you were often the last to know. There was another important difference; in the theater you might get good reviews and a little more money, but the world did not suddenly acclaim you,

With Maria Ouspenskaya (his teacher in the Group days) lunching in the Warner commissary

Julie and wife Roberta arriving in New York about 1939

your face did not appear on a thousand screens across the country, and mail did not arrive by the sackful at your doorstep. It was fantasy—the American dream of gold in the streets.

There were disagreements over what the Warners contract would mean to his career, so Julie and Roberta went to a lawyer to have it explained. In the end he signed, and they packed up and moved to Hollywood. Warner Brothers made pictures on the assembly line, and Garfield produced—four the first year, five the second. It was fame, money, and glamour, but it was also hard work—boring, laborious, sometimes monotonous. For a man whose life was acting, however, it was a total experience. It was a new life for John Garfield, and the name change completed the transformation. He was a new person called John Garfield.

John was a name that fit him like a tight shoe. "I'll always be Julie to my friends," he said. In the old days, Hollywood remade actors—they gave them new names and sometimes new faces. Garfield kept his face, but it was strange to hear him called Johnny. To the mass movie audience, however, he was John Garfield.

The next thing to become used to was the publicity—exaggerated stories about his life, sometimes like reading a synopsis of a studio script. Publicity would become a way of life when everyone knew his face. Box-office receipts went up or down on the basis of his popularity. But he could always go back to the theater; he had a clause in his contract permitting him to return to Broadway every other year.

In those first months of success he would say many idealistic things about the people who had helped him, about his love for the theater and acting. In fact, he did return to the New York stage in 1940 in the starring role of *Heavenly Express*. The reviews were good, but the play flopped. He didn't come back again until 1947. In between he made twenty-four films for Warner Bros. From 1938 to 1946 his main battle ground was on the studio lots, where he would fight for better scripts, better parts, and a bigger say in his choice of films. With each film he became more popular, his name better known.

He built a reputation as an actor who worked hard at his performances and was "the most democratic of star performers on the movie lots." He gave interviews to all the columnists and professed that he would never "go Hollywood." In New York, where a long-standing snobbery against Hollywood—some of it well founded —existed, Garfield was considered to be in the devil's grasp. A *New York Times* article lamented, "And thereby hangs the dilemma, for John Garfield has a serious mind. He works himself into a heavy lather over

With Hedda Hopper in their friendly days

the world's problems. He's a fine actor and that's what he wants to be. Can you imagine how he's going to feel when the director builds toward nothing more important than the Garfield smile that's going to make them happy."

Everyone was afraid Hollywood would spoil him. He, in turn, insisted that he was a stage actor, even when his impact in film was at its height. Those around him contributed to the bias, especially the old Group Theatre people—many of whom came to Hollywood through his help; Roberta, too, looked at the New York theater as a more serious place for an actor. When he finally did realize the tremendous power of the medium he worked in, he became totally committed to it, and he was one of the first actors to undertake independent film production.

In one sense the Warners years relate best to Garfield's personality in terms of an event that took place in 1949. He teamed that year with his old friend and alter ego Clifford Odets to star in the Broadway production of *The Big Knife*, billed as an exposé of Hollywood but, surely, more of a soul cleansing for the two men. Again, we must put aside the plot, for it is the emotional dilemma that was important to them. The play was both an act of colossal arrogance on their part and at the same time a serious attempt to expose their own failures and hypocrisies. Odets wrote it and Garfield played the lead, just as they had planned with the earlier *Golden Boy*. This time they dealt more directly with the emotional blunders and would-be ideals of their own lives. Garfield portrayed Charlie Castle, a film star trapped by his own desire to remain in a life that he knows is destroying him. His youthful ideals are shared by a faithful wife, whom he deeply cares for yet constantly betrays. In a sense this was their life made more dramatic and more elegant for the stage. Charlie Castle is part philosopher, part weakling, part humanist, part actor, and part hypocrite—a composite personality for Odets and Garfield.

After Garfield's death a thinly disguised fictionalized account would present unsympathetically the so-called sordid details of his life, but in a manner much inferior to that Garfield himself did on stage. The novel, *Prince Bart*, focused on his destructiveness, which was certainly a strong element in him. But Garfield beat the sensationalists at their own game, and he did it with more directness, on stage. Critics saw the play as a swipe at Hollywood, but it was certainly more of a swipe at the failings of author and star, as well as an apologia for what they hadn't accomplished.

These years marked many personal defeats for Garfield—a daughter born in 1938 died in 1945; his

The Garfields attending the premiere of Juarez *at Warners' Beverly Hills Theater*

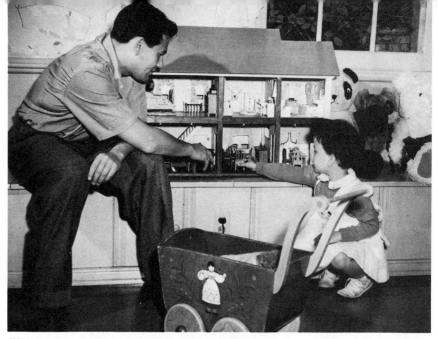

With daughter Katherine, who died suddenly in 1945

With daughter Katherine and newborn son David

25

Touring with the USO shows

relationship with his wife was embattled by his own growing popularity and notoriety; he found himself in many films that hardly seemed worth the effort, and his going on suspension didn't help. The clause in his contract that permitted him to return to the stage was used only once.

Politically he had crystallized his views behind FDR and the New Deal, while remaining sympathetic to the old New York radical ethic. He had always been a hero-worshiper, and FDR was a likely hero for him. He was overwhelmed with enthusiasm and excitement when he visited the White House and spent several hours with the President and his wife. He came to admire Eleanor Roosevelt as much as he did FDR.

Early interviews with Garfield are full of ideals and eagerness: "The pictures have been successes, but none of them have been important pictures." "I believe a little hardship is fine for the character." "My quarrels with the studio were never over money. All I wanted was good parts." The war years provided him with an opportunity to make up for the lack of important pictures with strenuous overseas duty. First drafted, then released because of his family, Garfield was on the first USO tour of American bases and an organizer of the Hollywood Canteen with Bette Davis; he even took a team to entertain Tito's partisans, when they were part of the Allied effort.

In 1943 an article appeared under his name entitled "Actors and Politics," in which he advocated full use of every actor in the war effort and, true to his American upbringing, noted that it was the duty of everyone, actors included, to participate in politics in a democracy. Professionally at least, by 1946 he was able to change the direction of his career. With the expiration of his Warners contract, Garfield set out as an independent producer of his own films.

This period is marked, on the one hand, by some of the best films and performances of his career and, on the other, with growing pressure and difficulties because of his political affiliations. Breaking with the studio was a significant act. No one simply declared himself a free agent—actors were something like baseball players, owned and traded by their studios. It was also difficult to get past the studio monopoly of equipment, actors, technicians, and distribution. Deals had to be negotiated through them, and only a few independents had succeeded. The big ones were Selznick and Goldwyn.

Garfield said enthusiastically to a columnist, "I've saved every penny I've earned here, and now I'm going to make the pictures I want to." He had been frugal with his money—loose with his living, perhaps, but money was an area he had dealt with surprisingly well. He had been a benefactor to New York theater friends who came to Hollywood, but he had saved his Warners

On one of the first USO tours, with Eddie Foy, Jr., next to him

earnings with foresight. Now he was turning down a lucrative salary offer from Warners to invest his own money in his talent. It was a gamble. With Bob Roberts as his producing partner, he joined Enterprise studio, a collection of writers, directors, and technicians who, like himself, were breaking away from the established system. Because of its political and working aspirations, Enterprise was an unusual experiment in filmmaking. Garfield was thus one of the originators of a movement that would overtake the industry in the next two decades.

For their first project they chose a story by Abraham Polonsky, who had one previous credit, at Paramount. The original screenplay, *Body and Soul*, bore resemblances to Odets's *Golden Boy* and to the whole genre of urban-ghetto living that had become Garfield's staple performance. However, the script varied the usual theme, about a man who sacrifices everything for the sake of material success, with potent doses of realism. The film was released through United Artists and was a critical and box-office success, alleviating Garfield's apprehensions about being on his own. It would be much easier to finance his next project. In fact, because he had taken a chance on an unknown writer and a writer turned director for his first venture, this success also confirmed his view that new and untried talent was available outside the Hollywood mills or laboring unknown within them.

1947 was probably his most satisfyingly productive year, the peak of his career and talent. *Body and Soul* was completed in the early part of the year; then he had a short bit in *Gentlemen's Agreement*, directed by his friend Elia Kazan from the Group Theatre; then he began another independent film, *Force of Evil*. Garfield and Roberts persuaded Abraham Polonsky to direct the new film, and a little-known New York actress, Beatrice Pearson, played the female lead. *Force of Evil* is the one Garfield film that has amassed a cult following over the years, mainly because of Polonsky's work and career. Critically acknowledged but ignored at the box office, it remains a strong story about corruption and success built on the values of the ghetto achiever striving for the new world of materialism.

In 1947 Garfield also returned to Broadway in the ANTA (American National Theater and Academy) production of *Skipper Next to God*, and he had finally achieved his goal of working simultaneously in both films and theater. In a year marked by success and intense work, he made one serious professional misjudgment. He was offered the part of Stanley Kowalski in Tennessee Williams's *A Streetcar Named Desire*. In fact, Irene Selznick issued a publicity release naming Garfield as the star in the new play. Suddenly,

With actress Virginia Grey and Naval war hero Morton Deitz prior to war bond drive on the East Coast

At a nightclub with Errol Flynn

With David Niven and Lilli Palmer

With Roberta; his only hobby was painting

Garfield withdrew from the project, stating that he felt the part of Kowalski was not important and was overshadowed by that of Blanche.

Later, he explained, "About *Streetcar*, the reason I didn't do it was just money. I think it is a great play. I wanted what I thought I was entitled to get. It was a commercial venture being put on for profit, and I wanted the same consideration as an Ingrid Bergman or a Spencer Tracy—I deserve that, I guess." Instead, he took an eighty-dollar-a-week role in the ANTA experimental production of *Skipper Next to God*. It was a play more to his liking, dealing with an important contemporary issue, while *Streetcar* was heavily immersed in passions and emotions. Obviously, Garfield was a natural for the part of Stanley Kowalski, but by withdrawing he opened the way for a little-known actor, Marlon Brando, to replace him. Garfield said of the part, "Stanley is more or less a repetition of the various leads I've played in movies. I wouldn't have been able to play it as good as Marlon Brando."

Garfield's return to the theater brought out another conflict in his professional work. From the first, those around him had claimed that the only real acting took place on the stage, in New York. In the early days in Hollywood, he insisted that he was a theater actor first. During that time it was common to downgrade filmwork, but in the long view, after seeing the impact of his rugged, immigrant features on screen, one realizes how little of this could come across on stage. He was remembered by many in the theater as an excellent comic actor, especially in his earlier days.

Although all the films he appeared in were not of consistent quality, in his Hollywood period he developed a single image on screen in a way that would not be achieved again. In fact, the very character he portrayed is now a facet of American history, and his various portrayals are the most complete fictional representation of it on film. His work adds a depth and understanding to the many books written about immigrant life in the city ghettos in the first half of the century.

For the next four years Garfield alternated between New York and Hollywood, appearing in three plays and four films. 1947 also marked a year of political difficulties for the motion picture industry. At first, because of his beliefs and his popularity and success, Garfield was an aggressive backer of liberal attempts to fight the congressional investigation of the industry. He joined the Committee for the First Amendment and spoke out against political repression. At the time there seemed no hint that he would be singled out as a prime target of what have come to be known as the "Hollywood witchhunts."

In 1949 he appeared in *The Big Knife*, by Clifford Odets. Political pressures were mounting against both Odets and Garfield, and the play stands out as a close examination of their own lives, defiant as well as guilt ridden, a last admission before the dream exploded for them both. His work the same year with John Huston on *We Were Strangers* seemed a mild attempt at political statement, but it came at a time when most of Hollywood was running for cover. In 1950 he appeared in Paul Green's adaptation of *Peer Gynt*. This was his most uncharacteristic role, a part that was outside the thrust of all his previous acting. It was a move he was obviously not prepared for, because it was the single most resounding flop of his career, panned by the critics, and closed after a short run.

Garfield's last three films, *The Breaking Point, Under My Skin*, and *He Ran All the Way,* were completed in the next two years. *The Breaking Point* and *He Ran All the Way* rank among the best work of his career. The latter is without doubt his single most impressive performance on film, and it was the last he would ever do.

In a way those last two years are filled with ironies, as is inevitable when one's life is bound up in political turmoil, emotional crisis, and business pressure. Garfield was in control of his own working energies and exercised good business sense; yet his very control isolated him from the people in power at the major studios who alone could give him protection from the congressional investigators. As a competitor to the studios, he was, in fact, a likely target. Ironically, had he accepted a new Warners contract (as Charlie Castle was forced to in Odets's play) he might have stayed in films, but the last several pictures he appeared in would never have been made.

Forced out of film work, he sought an outlet in New York. This time he was to perform in the play that had been indirectly responsible for his Hollywood success—*Golden Boy*. It would be his last acting performance. In it Garfield was reunited with former Group Theatre members, most of them also feeling the political hounds at their backs; Clifford Odets directed, and Lee J. Cobb, Joseph Wiseman, Art Smith, and Roman Bohnen were all in the cast. At a time when he should have been at the peak of his powers, he was being forced to retreat from audiences. Suddenly, the play about a man who loses his ideals, who capitulates to the material quest for fame and riches, whose physical strength leads him to spiritual disintegration, seemed totally within his grasp. His performance was powerful, and although some critics felt that the play had aged, all felt that Garfield's acting was ample compensation and had the ring of authenticity. By the

Studying a script at home

With Errol Flynn at the Warner's commissary

34

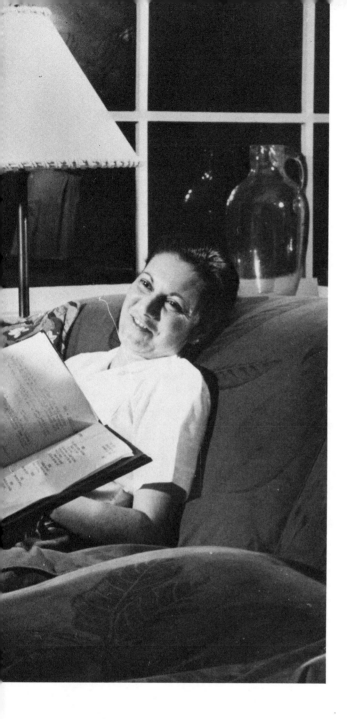

end of ten weeks' performance, Garfield was physically run-down and the photographs of him at this time show a tired and weary man. He had always appeared to be in top health, with a stocky build and a full head of hair, and as an avid tennis player, he was an unlikely candidate for a heart attack. But in 1947 he suffered his first attack while playing tennis.

It was a difficult blow to a man who prided himself on his physical appearance and in fact, had built a worldwide reputation on that appearance. He seemed incapable of recognizing its seriousness, but at least, he was able to ward off further attacks by adhering to a strict diet and schedule.

Garfield was not averse to high living. Hollywood romances were common publicity gimmicks during the thirties and forties, but the rumors that surrounded Garfield were not unfounded, and like his friend and mentor Odets, he was torn by conflicting moralities—on the one hand, his background of family and respectability, and on the other, his pure infatuation with success and the popularity and desirability that came with it. It is ironic that his contradiction was probably a source of great frustration to him. His affairs and liaisons increased as his difficulties became more serious, indicating that they were part of a pattern of self-destruction he had unconsciously outlined for himself in those last months. He was unemployable, business associates struck his name off their lists, former friends avoided him—he had become a nonperson. It is significant that the more oppressive his daily life became, the more intense were his self-destructive impulses.

In 1951 he appeared before the House Un-American Activities Committee, and while professing willingness to answer questions, he steadfastly refused to acknowledge Communist affiliation or to name anyone he might suspect of such ties. The committee wanted Garfield to be the first important, well-known celebrity to confess to past misconduct; he refused. What followed was a year of harassment by government agencies, lawyers, and self-professed patriotic organizations.

For the next year he was hemmed in on all sides and found himself fighting ideas, statements, allegations—a ground of combat he knew nothing about, for he had been an enthusiast, a devotee, not a thinker. He had been fiercely loyal to people, and when that loyalty was attacked he refused to give in. During those last months his success as an actor must have seemed a bitter mockery to him. He was being asked to choose between so-called loyalty to his country and loyalty to his friends.

During the last week of his life he was desperately

trying to clear himself from vague charges, going over old tax accounts and canceled checks, worrying about his wife's political affiliations, and at the same time, resisting the pressures that brought him closer to going back on the principles he had passionately believed in. He was also waging a physical battle—drinking, going without sleep, totally disregarding his own health. He quarreled with his wife, and in fact, he was frustrated by every action he took and by everyone close to him. In looking back, his wife has said, "I believe in fate, and he might have died anyway. But he wouldn't have died so angry. He was so angry." That anger was vented at everyone, but most of all at himself. When he died it was reported that he had not slept for two days.

He died on May 20, 1952, and the ironies persist. On May 19, Clifford Odets appeared before the House Un-American Activities Committee—his purpose, to come clean, admit membership in the Communist party, and name those of his friends who had been in it. Odets, too, felt himself at the end of the line. The two had worked together only a month before on *Golden Boy*, the play he had written for Garfield in the Group Theatre days. Odets had jokingly called the new production "Garfield's revenge." Despite the hard times and the difficulties they faced, their work together was a personal triumph for the two men. Part of its purpose must have been to buoy their spirits, to show that they could still perform even though conventional doors were closed to them. The play was a part of their personal drama, too. What Garfield must have thought when he knew Odets would name his friends, what this must have done to his own feelings of resistance, is difficult to estimate. Odets named several former Group Theatre members, and the following exchange took place on the afternoon of May 19.

MR. TAVENNER: Did John Garfield appear in the play?
MR. ODETS: Yes sir; he did.
MR. TAVENNER: Were you acquainted with John Garfield at that time?
MR. ODETS: Oh, yes.
MR. TAVENNER: Did you know John Garfield to be a member of the Communist party?
MR. ODETS: No, sir; I never knew.

That night, in the apartment of a former showgirl, Iris Whitney, John Garfield died of a heart attack at the age of thirty-nine. He died in his most characteristically self-destructive way—in a woman's apartment, estranged from his family, his idols crumbled, his faith gone.

Ironies persist. When his success seemed more brittle than ever, when his own weaknesses surfaced and aided his defeat, it was those very qualities that gave his last few performances their greatest strength. Particularly in his portrayal of men with glaring though human weaknesses, he was able to give a profound and moving performance.

From start to finish, like so many of our heroes, he lived the American dream—he had it all so suddenly and lost it just as quickly. We are drawn to that quality, to the unknown that bestows wealth with one hand and destroys with the other. We glorify the Deans and Monroes, the movie idols who are destroyed at the peak of their power. Of them all, Garfield seemed to be most genuine. He embodied more of our own qualities—ambition, hard-work ethic, pride, enthusiasm, weakness in the face of defeat. As an actor, he was always interesting, sometimes deeply moving, and throughout his career of real importance to his audience. As a person, he was intense, deeply attached to people, and very human.

Chapter 2: The Films

From his very first screen portrayal, John Garfield was a symbol for a large segment of the American population, but especially for the immigrant urban poor. As Julius Garfinkel he had shared their life, grown up and been nurtured in their streets. As John Garfield he was the romantic embodiment of all their dreams, and perhaps his own. These immigrant Europeans, who streamed into already crowded cities at the turn of the century, are the ancestors of the Blacks, Chicanos, and Puerto Ricans who have taken their place in the same tenements and streets.

All of them, yesterday and today, share common traits—they are outsiders, standing apart from the masses of the continent because they are on the bottom, fighting their way up or sometimes just fighting. For that earlier generation, John Garfield was their romantic image of themselves. He seemed an American in name only, a man whose parents could hardly speak the language, whose looks, manners, and values left him dangling on the fringe of society. His effect on these film audiences was explosive. It is much the same today when Blacks of the ghetto walk into a movie theater and see on the screen an actor who makes them say, "Yeah, that's the way I feel."

Garfield seemed to embody the urban poor's life experience in his looks, his voice, his gestures. His success at this characterization went beyond his skill as an actor and his formal training in the theater. It had more to do with his "film presence." He was not handsome in the Hollywood sense—his features were dark and Semitic, his nose appeared broken, and his accent was heavy Bronx with lower East Side shadings. No other film actor in 1938 who purported on screen to be an American looked so untypically American. His whole appearance said, "I just got here—and I'm staying!" It was the defiance of a generation pushing its way through the door.

This quality was fully exploited in Garfield's first screen role, the part of Mickey Borden in Warners' *Four Daughters*. The director, Michael Curtiz, was obviously aware of the potential Garfield offered the film. He used him judiciously, at times making him the focus of scenes where he had little direct involvement but where his presence dominated. Garfield himself credited the director with having established his film persona: "I would normally have been a character actor, but Mike Curtiz gave me the screen personality that carried me to stardom."

Garfield's popularity was instant and proved immensely important at the box office. Warner Bros. quickly capitalized on this, and in film after film that followed he was that same slum kid fighting to get from

With Mr. and Mrs. Jack Warner

the outside to the inside. How much of it was serious or true, or how much of it he believed in, is difficult to say. His own life proved to be a studio publicity man's dream. After all, wasn't Garfield a slum kid, a poor Jew from the ghetto who ran with street gangs and had to be reformed? Didn't he make it, and can't every kid who came up the same hard road make it? In a sense he was an illustration of how success could be a reality for ghetto achievers—undreamed-of success and dreamed-of glamour.

He knew the part well, and there were even times that he balked at playing another of what he called "disillusioned misanthropes" (but more often it was against a poor script rather than the characterization). When he was free of the studio and part owner of an independent producing company, he came back to the old theme—the slum kid breaking out—in such films as *Body and Soul* and *Force of Evil*. Now the story went deeper into the theme, and sometimes success was shown to be more corrupting than the slum streets. In the early films, it was simply a matter of boxing the champ, winning, and getting the girl, and the slum kid made the grade. In the later ones, winning sometimes meant moral defeat and losing the best part of your soul and retaining the worst.

Aside from one or two departures, that screen personality—the outsider—would be his mark on the American cinema. The way that character developed in his various films would prove in some ways a measure of the immigrant American's full view of himself and his success. For by the time Garfield died, in 1952, the generation he represented had become full-fledged members of the American middle class. World War II was their turning point; after it was over, the old goals —success and the American dream—would be achieved. Now the questioning and the doubts would set in.

It is interesting to take a close look at two films that give a clear view of the Garfield screen personality— one is the prewar *Dust Be My Destiny*, made in 1939; the other is the postwar *Force of Evil*, made in 1947. A comparison of the two films shows a significant change in the character of the downtrodden ghetto figure.

As Joe Bell in *Dust Be My Destiny*, Garfield is the victim of a society intent on punishing him, for no other reason than that he is poor and defiant. He has served a prison term under false arrest and then been thrown into a work camp for riding a freight illegally. Eventually, Joe Bell is redeemed with the aid of his

friends and justice, but not before he finds out what it is to be hunted and called a murderer. In this film it is the environment that victimizes the Garfield character; he is essentially good, but he has been cut off from opportunity. Change the social environment, says the story, and Joe Bell will be just like the rest of us.

In *Force of Evil*, the immigrant boy has already shed his physical environment, and only the mental marks remain. Now it is success he is after—not simply a modest job and happiness, but the biggest and the best. The corruption is within, and no longer can we point to poverty, blind justice, and poor conditions as the culprits. Garfield portrays a man whose every impulse has been corrupted by the values and goals that brought him out of the ghetto. His means of gaining his version of ultimate success involve a crooked plot to take over the numbers racket of the city. All the learned talents—the good ones, for isn't it every poor boy's dream to become a professional, a lawyer!—are put to an evil use. In carrying out his plan he must ruin his

With James Wong Howe and Claude Rains at the opening of Howe's restaurant

With Judy Garland at a rally for President Truman

brother and see his loyalties and desires shattered. In a final scene, after his brother has been killed, he chooses to destroy himself and the other thieves—his only redeeming act.

In both films, one a fairly idealized view of ghetto hardship and success, the other a stark glimpse at the ugly side of the same values, we see a fundamental change in attitude as well as in Garfield's persona. "Give me the opportunity!" the early films shouted. These films spoke in terms of achievement; the later ones questioned the means and the life one would lead during and after the quest.

Even in films where he had only a minor part, as in *Destination Tokyo* or *Gentlemen's Agreement,* Garfield portrayed that same struggling immigrant American. The quest for success did not have to be ruthless and violent; it could be as corrupting when he portrayed a struggling young violinist, as in the film *Humoresque.* Written by Clifford Odets, the story strongly resembles his play *Golden Boy.* Here, the corrupting influence of the world of culture outside the ghetto was given exposure. There are even shades of the same character in *Saturday's Children,* where Garfield portrays an unsuspecting office clerk who is trapped into marriage and out of his dreams of adventure, fame and fortune.

Another quality in his makeup also made these screen characters believable to the audience. Beyond the copy turned out by the publicity department and the corny stories concocted about his having been a boxer or the leader of a street gang or the graduate of a reform school, beyond all these exaggerations of the truth, Garfield was essentially an authentic representative of the people he characterized on the screen. His early life, as we have seen, was less spectacular and sensational than Hollywood made it appear, but it was still typical of the masses who lived in the urban ghettos, who were poor, who latched on to American values, and who pushed as hard as they could for success.

This sense of authenticity was an unusual quality in Hollywood. Garfield understood his parts with an unconscious ease—it is there in his walk, his flippancy, and his immense energy. That energy could be a powerful force when controlled by a director; often, he was allowed to let it spill into a part, and then he shouted and postured. But when a director recognized his qualities and realized that sometimes an effect could become more powerful if Garfield was not allowed to burst out of the role—then he could give the kind of realistic performance that few actors could equal.

THE WARNER YEARS

As a contract player for a major Hollywood studio, Garfield was part of a large organization, and his films were handled as a marketable product. How, then, could one actor maintain so consistent a figure in all his films? The answer is simple. The industry based its decisions on box-office receipts; if a product did well, they argued, make it again with the same actor, etc. At its worst, this attitude could result in an assembly-line product that would make Detroit look creative. At its best, it provided a permanent repertory company of actors, directors, writers, scene designers, makeup men, etc. In some sense it was an ideally secure arrangement for a working actor. Few periods in the history of the theater could equal it for financial stability. Of course, it was not ideal, and one had to fight to get the right parts and to keep from being shunted from film to film like a slave.

In Garfield's case, he waged an ongoing war with Warner Bros. and was suspended at least a dozen times for refusing to work with inferior and repetitious material. The studio—at that time one of its specialties was the "social documentary" style, dealing with the middle and lower classes—fitted in well with the screen image Garfield would represent. He obviously would have been used differently at, say, MGM, a studio he worked for and is thought to have liked. Producers at Warners could order a "Garfield vehicle" from the writers and directors, who knew immediately what was wanted.

Through the studio-repertory system, Garfield worked with several people over the years who influenced his development as an actor as well as his screen image. Michael Curtiz, if not his discoverer, was at least the first to tap his potential. Garfield made *Four Daughters, Daughters Courageous, The Sea Wolf,* and *The Breaking Point* with Curtiz, and all are good stories, each adding a new dimension to the Garfield screen personality. The first two films were most important in establishing him as the urban underdog. *The Sea Wolf,* while giving Garfield another role as a rebel, was really Edward G. Robinson's film. In the work with Curtiz, Garfield is always restrained, his acting flaws held in check by the director. Curtiz was effective in getting the best performances from actors, and he had an ability in casting parts that suited the actor visually as well as emotionally. In *The Breaking Point,* Garfield gave one of his best performances as the rebel hanging on to nothing and willing to do anything

to keep it. Garfield was now a more mature actor, and his portrayal of a strong man with glaring weaknesses just below the surface was particularly perceptive.

Another influence on the Garfield screen character was writer-director Robert Rossen. Rossen wrote three early Garfield films, *Dust Be My Destiny, Out of the Fog,* and *The Sea Wolf.* He later directed Garfield's independent production of *Body and Soul.* In the first two films, Rossen went a long way in fixing the standard Garfield character—Joe Bell in *Dust Be My Destiny* and a small time waterfront racketeer in *Out of the Fog.* In his directorial effort with Garfield, Rossen was in familiar territory. *Body and Soul* revived the cliché of the kid who boxes his way out of the ghetto, but it also gave a visually hard-hitting view of the seamy life of its protagonists. From an original screenplay by Abraham Polonsky, the film presented a closer look at the ghetto myth and the victims of its values. Polonsky, by way of this screenplay and his later work as director and co-author of *Force of Evil,* was influential in delineating a more mature view of the Garfield ghetto figure and his battle with success.

Another early influence on the Garfield screen personality was the writing team of Julius J. and Philip G. Epstein, who wrote some of the wittiest dialogue to come out of Hollywood in the thirties and forties. In *Four Daughters* and *Daughters Courageous,* they established a brand of fast-talking cynical repartee for him. Their specialty of humor with a heavy dose of cynicism afforded Garfield's rebel figure a comic self-parodying stance rarely developed in his other films. With *Saturday's Children* they were able to translate the play to the screen with sharp comic overtones.

There were others who influenced Garfield's acting abilities and training, but they belong more properly to his early work in the theater. Although the content of the films sometimes did not live up to his acting abilities, taken as a whole, they show a very impressive list of work. He made thirty-one films in thirteen years, a busy schedule, coupled with at least a half dozen new stage performances in New York and Hollywood. He was described as a man who could not relax, a man who had to work. His acting was the center of his life, and in each of his film roles, he seems to have given that extra dimension of performance—a combination of work, energy, and inspiration that could make a line or gesture better than it seemed.

In the Shanghai Lil *sequence*

FOOTLIGHT PARADE
1933

Director, Lloyd Bacon, *script*, Manuel Seff and James Seymour; *dance director*, Busby Berkeley; *music and lyrics*, Harry Warren, Al Dubin, Sammy Fain, and Irving Kahal; *cameraman*, George Barnes; *editor*, George Amy; *released, September 1933; running time,* 100 minutes; Warner Bros.

CAST: James Cagney, Joan Blondell, Ruby Keeler, Dick Powell, Guy Kibbee, Ruth Donnelly, Claire Dodd, Hugh Herbert, Frank McHugh, Gordon Wescott, Renee Whitney, Philip Faversham, Juliet Ware, Herman Bing, Paul Porcasi, William Granger, Charles Wilson, Barbara Rogers, Jules Garfield (*as a sailor*).

At the age of nineteen, Garfield had hitchhiked west and landed in Hollywood. In the early thirties, Hollywood was the goal of every romantic young man and woman. It promised instant glamour, success, riches. Garfield seems to have given Hollywood a very short fling and probably had no intention of remaining there; his sights had always been set on the New York stage, which seemed a better outlet to someone who took acting seriously.

His ten-second bit in *Footlight Parade* was prophetic, since it was done at Warners and involved many people he would later work with in films. *Footlight Parade* was one of the first of the Warners musical extravaganzas. Garfield's closeup comes in the third reel, during a Cagney dance number in a barroom amid sailors and Oriental bargirls. Garfield appears after a choreographed fight in which tables and chairs are thrown and everyone runs for cover; his head peeks from behind a table looking very young and wide-eyed.

Several months later he was back in New York. He would not return to Hollywood until 1938.

With Priscilla Lane

FOUR DAUGHTERS
1938

Director, Michael Curtiz; *producer,* Hal B. Wallis;
associate producer, Benjamin Glazer; *script,* Julius J.
Epstein and Lenore Coffee, from *Sister Act,* by Fannie
Hurst; *art director,* John Hughes; *musical score,* Max
Steiner; *cameraman,* Ernie Haller; *editor,* Ralph
Dawson; *released September 24, 1938; running time,*
90 minutes; Warner Bros.

CAST: John Garfield, Priscilla Lane, Rosemary Lane,
Lola Lane, Claude Rains, Jeffrey Lynn, Gale Page,
Frank McHugh, May Robson, Dick Foran, Vera Lewis,
Tom Dugan, Eddie Acuff, Donald Kerr.

This is the film role that literally made Garfield an
overnight star—the part of Mickey Borden, a brash,
sardonic misfit from the city thrust into the middle of

beautiful American small-town life. Garfield outshone,
outquipped, and outsmoked everyone in the cast. His
presence brought to the story a sense of reality that had
a striking effect within the essentially fantasized view of
the average American small-town family. With a very
shrewd dramatic sense of Garfield's abilities and his
physical forcefulness in front of the camera, Curtiz was
able to lift a witty but rather pedestrian script above its
literal meaning.

The description of Mickey Borden would fit the
Garfield image for many future films: "His dress is
shabby, but he is fortunate that his carelessness adds to
his attractiveness. His manner is indolent, his expression
wry, almost surly. His humor is ironic. When he smiles
(which is seldom) his demeanor is sardonic. Mickey
Borden doesn't think well of himself or the world.
Poverty has done the trick." Garfield was Borden! He
later said that he had patterned his characterization

after a pianist he had known from New York—Oscar Levant. If so, he caught Levant's verbal style expertly, but his physical style was uniquely his own—shabbiness also looked good on Jules Garfield, giving him a defiant air.

Carelessness was becoming to him too. Sitting at the piano, cigarette dangling from the corner of his mouth, hat on head, hair disheveled, he plays his music—a piece without a beginning or an end. When Priscilla Lane, who has been secretly listening, says, "It's beautiful," he peeks at her from below his eyelids and replies, "It stinks!" From that moment, he won the audience.

Venerable old May Robson offers him a cup of tea, and he growls at her, "You needn't look so noble; tea is only a little hot water." He was punching little holes in the fantasy of the story, the kind of holes his audience —living in the depression—would have poked in this idyllic portrayal of middle-class American life.

A combination of events made his success in the film possible. Essentially, he was right for the medium; he was a natural. The Borden role would utilize the best features of his acting style—his defiant, brash delivery, which seemed to emphasize his New York accent rather than cover it, his ability to deliver a good comic line, and of course, his physical presence. In *Four Daughters*, Curtiz called on all these abilities and used them well. Even though he lost the girl and drove off into a snowstorm, never to be heard from again, Garfield the actor would be heard of for some time to come.

Synopsis:

When Jeffrey Lynn comes to the house of a music professor (Claude Rains) to board, the professor's four daughters immediately fall in love with him. The youngest daughter (Priscilla Lane) captures him, and they are to be married. But when she learns from Mickey Borden (John Garfield) that her sister is broken-hearted over her marriage, she runs off with Borden. Her sacrifice is useless, for her former fiancé goes away, and her sister realizes that she loves another. Finally, Garfield, too, sees that he has come between the intended lovers, and he drives his car over a cliff in a snowstorm. The lovers are tentatively reunited at the end.

With Jeffrey Lynn

50

With Eddie Acuff, Don Kerr, Tom Dugan and Priscilla Lane

Reviews:

The New York Times,
August 19, 1938:

Four Daughters is one of the best pictures of anybody's career, if only for the sake of the marvelously meaningful character of Mickey Borden as portrayed by John (formerly Jules) Garfield, who bites off his lines with a delivery so eloquent that we still aren't sure whether it is the dialogue or Mr. Garfield who is so bitterly brilliant. Our vote, though, is for Mr. Garfield, and for whatever stars watch over his career on the stage and screen, because, on re-reading the dialogue, as we have just done carefully, it seems to have lost something of the acidity, the beautiful clarity it had when Mr. Garfield spoke it. . . . Mr. Garfield, with a cigarette dangling from his mouth, no money, not even a clean shirt, a personal grudge against the Fates, an interesting vocabulary and a heart of purest suet—Mr. Garfield, the eternal outsider.

Variety,

Garfield develops a great character with consummate artistry, compelling a fascinating interest from his first to last scenes.

51

Newsweek,
August 29, 1938:

John Garfield steals the acting honors with his realistic portrayal of doomed pessimism. . . . The cast is rather remarkable in that three of its most important roles have been assigned to newcomers. All three are performers of considerable promise. Gale Page made her screen debut a few months ago. . . . Jeffrey Lynn was lost in a bit part in "Cowboy from Brooklyn." John Garfield, a graduate of New York's Group Theatre, has never appeared on the screen before and is undoubtedly the outstanding film find of the year.

The New Yorker,
August 27, 1938:

Just as we have adjusted our senses to a generally amiable, good-natured comedy of the gentle sentiments . . . the door opens and this young man of lowering aspect, a mean and embittered wastrel ambles in and distracts us entirely from the nice things of life. . . . He's John (formerly Jules) Garfield, whom most of us saw on the stage in "Having Wonderful Time," but I don't recall that he displayed any such vigor, agreeable as he was there, as he does before the camera.

Between Priscilla Lane and May Robson

With Claude Rains as a cop trailing Garfield

THEY MADE ME A CRIMINAL
1939

Director, Busby Berkeley; *producer*, Jack L. Warner; *associate producer*, Benjamin Glazer; *script*, Sig Herzig, from a story by Bertram Millhauser and Beulah Marie Dix; *cameraman*, James Wong Howe; *editor*, Jack Killifer; *released, January 28, 1939; running time, 92 minutes*; Warner Bros.

CAST: John Garfield, Claude Rains, Ann Sheridan, May Robson, Gloria Dickson, Robert Gleckler, John Ridgely, Barbara Pepper, William Davidson, Billy Halop, Bobby Jordan, Leo Gorcey, Huntz Hall, Gabriel Dell, Ward Bond, Robert Strange, Frank Riggi, Cliff Clarke, Dick Wessel, Raymond Brown, Sam Hayes.

PRICES
RINGSIDE $3.30
GEN. ADM. 1.10
GALLERY .5

With Gloria Dickson

With the Dead End Kids and Gloria Dickson

With Joe Downing (left)

56

This was a Warners remake of an earlier successful film, *The Life of Jimmy Dolan*, but it is a straightforward treatment of an entertaining story with some excellent action direction. Director Busby Berkeley was making his last film under Warners contract and also departing from the series of highly successful musical extravaganzas that have become synonymous with his name. He showed that he knew just what qualities in the young Garfield to exploit. The realistically enacted boxing sequences come off particularly well, and cameraman James Wong Howe would work with Garfield several years later using even greater realism in the boxing ring on the film *Body and Soul*.

One of the most striking action sequences in the film begins as a frolicsome and harmless swim in an irrigation tank, until the water is let out—enough to keep the boys from getting out but not enough to let them rest and stop swimming. It is a strikingly visual scene, done with mounting tension and suspense.

With Garfield are the Dead End Kids, who, like himself, were depression-style juvenile delinquents, brash, boyish misfits from the city ghettos, authentic representatives of their class. Like him, they were often given inferior material that was sometimes offset by their enthusiasm and dynamism. Eventually, they wound up doing second-grade material entirely (still the Dead End Kids, even though they were all in their late twenties and early thirties). Fortunately Garfield was able, by fighting for his career, to avoid their fate.

This was a successful film, but Garfield was anxious for a variety of parts. He was also finding out that film work could be physically exhausting; the movie was shot in the Palm Desert, where the intense heat could melt the film in the camera and the gnats forced the crew (except the actors, of course) to wear netting. The only sour note in the film was the necessary upbeat ending which worked against the facts of the story and the character. Nevertheless, this was one of Garfield's most natural performances.

Synopsis:

Johnny Burns (John Garfield) faces a false murder charge the night after a drunken brawl given to celebrate his winning the lightweight championship. Forced to leave town, he rides the freights out west and lands at a desert date ranch run by two women. They are having a struggle to keep the ranch going and support the six young New York ruffians whom they are trying to regenerate.

Having fallen in love with the young owner, Johnny Burns enters a prize-fight contest to get money to help the ranch. This puts Detective Phelon on his trail, since he recognizes Johnny's unusual boxing stance. Johnny realizes that if he fights he will be imprisoned. At first he wants to run away, but he decides to get the money and face Phelon. When he is about to be taken back, the policeman relents and lets Johnny return to the ranch and obscurity.

Review:

The New York Times,
January 21, 1939

If you repeat the title of the new picture *They Made Me a Criminal*—you can almost fancy you hear the voice of John Garfield accusing the Warner Brothers. . . . So now they've made John Garfield a criminal, and since Mr. Garfield is young, resilent and no end talented, he is making the best of what, after all, is not such a bad situation. . . . It is always Mr. Garfield with his sublime self-confidence, the unhandsome attractiveness of his greasy, round, gamin face, who carries the show along.

As a hotshot reporter

BLACKWELL'S ISLAND
1939

Director, William McGann; *script*, Crane Wilbur, from a story by Crane Wilbur and Lee Katz; *released, March 25, 1939; running time,* 71 minutes; Warner Bros.

CAST: Victor Jory, Rosemary Lane, John Garfield, Dick Purcell, Stanley Fields, Morgan Conway, Granville Bates, Anthony Averill, Peggy Shannon, Charles Foy, Norman Willis, Joe Cunningham.

Blackwell's Island ranks as a throwaway film for Garfield. He had started production on it before the release and subsequent success of his performance in *Four Daughters*. He reported in one newspaper, "We had been shooting the film for ten days, when someone in the higher echelons of Warners said, 'What's Garfield doing in that film?' " The studio sent in Michael Curtiz as director and tried desperately to boost the part of their newfound star.

With Leon Ames, Rosemary Lane and Joe Cunningham

With Stanley Fields

Although the story was based on an authentic incident, the famous raid by Austin MacCormick on Welfare Island prison in 1934, the film never caught a coherent style to present the facts—it tried to mix broad comedy, satire, and some authentic prison backgrounds. Actually, it is quite obvious that Garfield's role had little to do with the main part of the story. He plays a Ben Hecht–style reporter boosting his career on the fortunes of the gangster played by Stanley Fields. He seems to appear in the most unlikely sequences, even able to get himself thrown into prison to report on corrupt doings.

Synopsis:

Reporter Tim Hayden (John Garfield) brings to light the activities of gangster Bull Branson (Stanley Fields) and is instrumental in sending him to prison. Investigating rumors that the prison is run by the inmates through corrupt politicians, Garfield has himself sentenced there for a short term. In prison, Branson attempts to kill him. Garfield escapes and reveals what is going on inside. The district attorney then leads a raid on the island.

Review:

The New York Times,
March 2, 1939:

Well, it's sound melodrama nevertheless and amusing, too, in a cynical way. . . . The really fictional trimmings are decorative enough. John Garfield as the reporter out to expose the crime ring, Stanley Fields as the moronic public enemy, Granville Bates as the spineless warden and usual melodramatic windowdressing. It seems almost too Hollywood to be true, but, since most of it is, we New Yorkers will have to grin and admit that the laugh is on us.

As Porfirio Diaz, with Paul Muni as Juarez

JUAREZ
1939

Director, William Dieterle; *producer,* Hal B. Wallis; *associate producer,* Henry Blanke; *script,* John Huston, Wolfgang Reinhardt, and Aeneas MacKenzie, from *Phantom Crown,* by Franz Werfel and Betito Harding; *art director,* Anton Grot; *music director,* Leo F. Forbstein; *cameraman,* Tony Gaudio; *editor,* Warren Low; *released, June 10, 1939; running time, 132 minutes;* Warner Bros.

CAST: Paul Muni, Bette Davis, Brian Aherne, John Garfield, Donald Crisp, Joseph Calleia, Gale Sondergaard, Gilbert Roland, Henry O'Neill, Pedro de Cordoba, Montague Love, Harry Davenport, Walter Fenner, Alex Leftwick, Bill Wilkerson.

With Brian Aherne

With Joseph Calleia, Martin Garralaga, and Paul Muni

With *Juarez*, Garfield finally portrayed a totally different character; yet in some ways, the film and the part were a disaster for him. In particular, his accent worked against him; it was a flaw that could be used to advantage in his familiar roles, but in a different setting, especially a historical one, it undermined his acting. Also, the director did not control Garfield's sometimes overenergetic style. In the role of Porfirio Díaz, the revolutionary general to Juárez, Garfield's bursting energy drained the character of realism. He relied on a fast-paced, excitable delivery for his speeches. Either the director was saddled with making the best of a precast movie or he didn't know how to use Garfield to advantage.

As with many epic-style historical productions, this film combined fanciful personal details with large (though not too complex) philosophical questions. In this case, the philosophical issues are the love between Maximilian and Carlota, and Juárez's burning desire to bring democracy (American style) to Mexico.

The whole temper of the film is didactic; in fact, Garfield's first two speeches are pure expounding, and he is more a mouthpiece than a person. As written, the part seems to have prevented him from coming to an understanding of the character.

But he was exceedingly happy to be involved with the film; it gave him a chance to work with some of the

prestige actors on the Warners lot, and Paul Muni, who had done biographical films on Zola and Pasteur, was considered one of the best character actors of the time.

Synopsis:

An elaborate epic of three interwoven plots involving the intrigue of Napoleon III to bring Mexico under France's rule; the tragic romance between Maximilian, Napoleon's appointed Emperor of Mexico, and Carlota; and the political fortunes of Benito Juárez, who seeks to liberate Mexico from foreign rule and monarchy and set up a democracy.

Review:

The New York Times,
April 26, 1939:

Mr. Dieterle yet must answer the charge that he has taken advantage of the remarkable stage presence of the Messrs. Muni, Aherne, Garfield and Rains to mount them, recurrently, on metaphoric soap boxes for purposes of declamation.

With Claude Rains

DAUGHTERS COURAGEOUS
1939

Director, Michael Curtiz; *producer,* Hal B. Wallis;
associate producer, Henry Blanke; *script:* Julius J.
and Philip C. Epstein, from a story by Dorothy
Bennett and Irving White; *cameraman,* James Wong
Howe; *editor,* Ralph Dawson; *released, July 22, 1939;
running time,* 107 minutes; Warner Bros.

CAST: John Garfield, Claude Rains, Priscilla Lane,
Rosemary Lane, Lola Lane, Gale Page, Jeffrey Lynn,
Fay Bainter, Donald Crisp, May Robson, Frank
McHugh, Dick Foran.

With Priscilla Lane

With George Humbert, Fay Bainter, Priscilla Lane, and Berton Churchill

Garfield received top billing in this remake of the *Four Daughters* theme, but the script, by the Epstein brothers, put the emphasis on comedy and satire instead of the melodrama of the earlier version. Garfield's characterization has lost the harsh grimness of Mickey Borden, and a wry, cocky smile was substituted for Borden's despairing sneer. In his very first scene, he is in front of a judge for practicing his con man's art in public. Fay Bainter, mother of the four daughters, is there to help Garfield as a favor to his lower-class-immigrant father. Watching is a wide-eyed, fascinated Priscilla Lane. Garfield turns to her and says, "I want her for my lawyer." Priscilla Lane follows him around like a puppy dog, and a few minutes later as they walk down the street, Garfield looks deeply into her wide eyes and asks, "Wanna buy me a beer?"

Although following a well-tried Hollywood formula, "remake your successes," *Daughters Courageous* was a likable and amusing film. Curtiz was able to utilize Garfield's comic delivery with effectiveness. Garfield had used this ability in the theater but would not have much opportunity to perfect it for the next decade. The film was also enhanced by excellent performances from the cast of *Four Daughters* fame, especially Claude Rains, a versatile character actor of the period.

Synopsis:

Deserting his wife and daughters to keep a rendezvous with the universe, Claude Rains returns home just as his ex-wife is about to marry a steady and respectable businessman (Donald Crisp). The vagabond father's charm all but upsets the situation. At first hostile, the daughters soon warm to their father. Priscilla Lane, as the youngest daughter, decides to marry John Garfield, who portrays a young man very much like her father and seems headed for a similar life. The two vagabonds become friends, and they decide to leave together on their date with the universe, before they do too much damage.

Review:

The New York Times,
June 24, 1939:

Once again John Garfield, the fatalistic interloper, is on the outside looking in and ultimately paying the penalty of his nonconformism. . . . In Mr. Garfield's case, at least, the role's concept shrieks of attempted duplication.

With Priscilla Lane and Stanley Ridges in the front while the Dead End Kids occupy the roof

With Ward Bond

DUST BE MY DESTINY
1939

Director, Lewis Seiler; *script,* Robert Rossen and Arthur J. Odlum; *editor,* Warren Lowe; *cameraman,* James Wong Howe; *released, September 16, 1939. running time,* 88 minutes; Warner Bros.

CAST: John Garfield, Priscilla Lane, Stanley Ridges, Alan Hale, Billy Halop, Charlie Grapewin, Frank McHugh, Henry Armetta, John Litel, Bobby Jordan, Moroni Olsen, Victor Killian, Frank Jaquet, Marc Lawrence, George Irving.

With Bobby Jordan and Billy Halop

This was one of three "crime" films Warners packaged for Garfield during 1938 and 1939 in an attempt to add him to their roll-call of "gangster types." *Dust Be My Destiny* had all the earmarks of the well-worn Warners vehicle—the story of a street boy who becomes a criminal because society and his environment are against him. Of his five films, four had offered this same characterization for Garfield.

The script involved the rambling escapades of the hero and his girlfriend, which had some resemblance to the real-life activities of the legendary Bonnie and Clyde. The film is notable as one of the first of a series dealing with that subject. But it departs from real-life facts in following the young pair from crisis to crisis until society, in the form of a benevolent judge and jury, finally rights the wrongs it has done to Joe Bell and his girlfriend.

It is safe to assume that *Dust Be My Destiny* was one of the parts that prompted Garfield to buck the studio executives and be suspended. He argued for better and more varied roles, and Warners came up with more gangster stories. He had been suspended before, and the studio was not about to give in; at least, they were willing to prove that their young, volatile star was wrong.

With Billy Halop and Bobby Jordan

With Priscilla Lane

71

Synopsis:

Joe Bell (John Garfield) is released from prison after serving a sentence for a crime he didn't commit. Bitter and frustrated, he is soon arrested for vagrancy and sent to a country work farm. Here he meets Mabel, the stepdaughter of the drunken farm foreman. Joe and Mabel fall in love and are discovered by the foreman. A fight between Joe and the foreman results in the latter's death from a heart attack. The two young people run away, believing they will be held responsible for the death.

Believing Joe caused the foreman's death, the police pursue the couple. Joe and Mabel lead the life of fugitives, always forced to flee when they are found out. In a last chance, Mabel realizes the futility of their plight and turns Joe in to the police. At the trial, the prosecutor accuses Joe of murder. The defense attorney makes a sympathetic and sentimental plea for Joe Bell as a symbol of all the down-and-out men and women who roam the country. He asks for a second chance for them all. Joe is cleared of the charge, and he and Mabel are freed.

Review:

The New York Times,
October 7, 1939:

John Garfield, official gall-and-wormwood taster for the Warners, is sipping another bitter brew . . . in *Dust Be My Destiny*, latest of the brothers' apparently interminable line of melodramas about fate-dogged boys from the wrong side of the tracks. . . . We detect signs in Mr. Garfield of taking even his cynicism cynically and of weariness in Miss Lane at having to redeem Mr. Garfield all over again.

With Anne Shirley

SATURDAY'S CHILDREN
1940

Director, Vincent Sherman; *producers,* Jack L. Warner and Hal B. Wallis; *associate producer,* Henry Blanke; *script,* Julius J. and Philip G. Epstein, from the play by Maxwell Anderson; *cameraman,* James Wong Howe; *editor,* Owen Marks; *released, May 11, 1940; running time,* 101 minutes; Warner Bros.

CAST: John Garfield, Anne Shirley, Claude Rains, Lee Patrick, Roscoe Karns, George Tobias, Berton Churchill, Dennis Moore, Elizabeth Risdon, Tom D'Andrea.

With Anne Shirley in scene cut from the film

With Anne Shirley, Tom Dugan, and John Qualen

With Anne Shirley

Saturday's Children was something of a victory for Garfield. It was his prize after repeated battles with the Warners executives for a variety of acting parts that broke away from the stereotyped crime film. But the victory was momentary, for the film was a box-office flop and prompted the executives to say, "See, we told you it wouldn't work; the public won't accept you in that role."

The role was that of a young city boy caught in a web of marriage and love that thwarts his outlandish dreams of adventure, invention, and the Philippines. The setting was pure Odets, and the comedy bore the satirical stamp of the Epstein brothers. The original play by Maxwell Anderson had been a success and had even been made into an earlier film version. But Garfield gave a convincing performance of the naïve and gullible young man who needs to have others, particularly the young girl who wants to marry him, make decisions for him. Together they seem to build a web of frustration and entanglement that almost engulfs them.

With Anne Shirley and George Tobias

It is a sensitive and touching film. Garfield mustered all his boyish qualities to bring the naïveté of the boy off and succeeded in making him wide-eyed, somewhat stupid, but extremely lovable. There are some good comic touches, particularly one with Tom D'Andrea as a cab driver following the young couple down the street, attempting to coerce them into using his cab (a good glimpse at the depression years, also), and another involving a drunk scene between Garfield and his brother-in-law, played by Roscoe Karns, where they lament the trap they have been caught in.

Unfortunately, the film has been forgotten. It would have direct meaning to an audience today, and Garfield's portrayal is fresh and understanding.

Synopsis:

An average New York family tries to make ends meet during the depression, snatching their moments together between subway rush hours. The youngest daughter, Bobby, has started work with her father at the office where he is a clerk. She meets Rimes Rosson (John Garfield), a shy young inventor, and their romance flourishes at the bowling alley and company dances.

Rimes wants to go to the Philippines to seek his fortune, and when a job offer (paying enough for one) comes through, he is given a farewell party by his co-workers. Bobby feels both frustrated and confused by Rimes's action, and against her instinct, she allows her sister to help her trap Rimes into marriage. To her dismay, the trap works, and the young couple try to make a home. But war and high prices are against them, and they are forced to fall back on the family.

Rimes feels trapped, and when he learns how he was tricked into marriage, he decides to accept the Philippine offer without his wife. Bobby's father makes a desperate attempt to bring the couple together. Finally, the two young people admit their past mistakes and, though uncertain, decide to remain together.

Review:

The New York Times,
May 4, 1940:

No studio in Hollywood seems to have a more consistent regard for the American middle class, with its myriad sorrows and triumphs, its domestic delights and decisions, than Warner Brothers. . . . But particular praise is in store for John Garfield, the sallow Romeo with the sad face and troubled soul, who falls into the part of the harassed young lover as though it had been written for him alone.

With Elizabeth Risdon, Claude Rains, Roscoe Karns,
Lee Patrick and Anne Shirley

With Roscoe Karns, Lee Patrick, and Anne Shirley

Embracing Ann Sheridan; Lee Phelps is the guard

CASTLE ON THE HUDSON
1940

Director, Anatole Litvak; *associate producer*, Samuel Bishoff; *script*, Seton I. Miller, Brown Holmes, and Courtney Terrett, from the book *20,000 Years in Sing Sing*, by Lewis E. Lawes; *cameraman*, Arthur Edeson; *editor*, Thomas Richards; *released, July 15, 1940; running time*, 75 minutes; Warner Bros.

CAST: John Garfield, Ann Sheridan, Pat O'Brien, Burgess Meredith, Henry O'Neill, Guinn Williams, Jerome Cowen, John Litel, Margot Stevenson, Willard Robertson, Edward Pauley, Billy Wane, Nedda Harrigan, Wade Boteler, Barbara Pepper, Robert Strange.

With Ann Sheridan, Jerome Cowan, and Willard Robertson

With Robert E. Homans, Emmett Vogan, and Tom Jackson

81

With Burgess Meredith

Ann Sheridan pleads with warden Pat O'Brien

This film was a virtual verbatim remake of *20,000 Years in Sing Sing*, which starred Spencer Tracy and was directed by Michael Curtiz. It was a huge success the first time for Warners and propelled Tracy to stardom. It was certainly part of their plan for Garfield —to build his image as a tough gangster type. One interesting aspect of the film was its literal copying of the earlier version; in fact, some of the backgrounds look identical.

Another interesting similarity is that neither Tracy nor Garfield is totally believable as the toughened gangster who stands by his word. This was a role that Cagney, Bogart, or Robinson, with their angular hardness, could have brought off with utter believability, but Tracy and Garfield possessed a certain physical softness, perhaps weakness, that made them less than ideal for the part. Garfield always seemed best able to represent a brooding personality; his most effective shot was a close-up, with the camera tight on him as he gazed out into space, an intense frown curving over the lines of his face.

Synopsis:

Tommy Gordon (John Garfield) is an arrogant gangster whose one weakness is his love for Kay (Ann Sheridan). He is sent to jail, where he meets Warden Lord (Pat O'Brien). The warden tries to help Tommy, and when a prison break occurs, Tommy does not join because Saturday is his unlucky day. Soon he is trusted by the warden and shows signs of changing.

When Kay is seriously injured in a car crash, the warden lets Tommy leave prison to visit her on his promise to return immediately. At Kay's apartment he learns that his crooked lawyer is responsible for her accident. When the lawyer arrives, the two fight, and Kay shoots the lawyer. She persuades Tommy to leave, and he is soon sought for murder. But he returns to prison to save the warden and goes to the electric chair, shielding Kay from a murder charge.

Review:

The New York Times,
March 4, 1940:

This is merely a routine notice that Mr. John Garfield, formerly of the Group Theatre, who was recently sentenced to a term in Warner Brothers pictures, is still in prison. . . .

Mr. Garfield, who seems to be wearing a little thin, for some reason—can it be possible that he has been a trifle over built as a screen personality—is the tough but golden-hearted prisoner who goes to the death house trailing wisecracks like cigarette ashes.

With three of Warners' toughest guys: G. Pat Collins, William Haade, and Dutch Hendrian

FLOWING GOLD
1940

Director, Alfred Green; *associate producer*, William Jacobs; *script*, Kenneth Gamet, from the story by Rex Beach; *cameraman*, Sid Hickok; *editor*, James Gibbon; *released, August 28, 1940, running time,* 82 minutes, Warner Bros.

CAST: John Garfield, Frances Farmer, Pat O'Brien, Raymond Walburn, Cliff Edwards, Tom Kennedy, Granville Bates.

With Pat O'Brien

With Pat O'Brien

In some ways, this film was an attempt to cash in on the success of *Boom Town*, which starred Tracy and Gable at MGM. It is set in the oil fields of the West, with two tough working men and the woman they both love as the center of the story. But Garfield's character is different. He is a man on the run from the law, and the opening scene in the mud streets of an oil town is an excellent visual representation of the Garfield character and his inability to trust any situation or any other person. By now also, the women in Garfield's films have been given recognizable characteristics—tough working girls able to handle themselves with wisecracks or in a man's world doing a man's job. Here Frances Farmer, another fugitive from the Group Theatre (she played opposite Luther Adler in *Golden Boy*), plays the tough but feminine woman for whom Garfield must fight and redeem himself.

The film was another success at the box office and went a long way in establishing the kind of part Warner executives wanted for Garfield. He would have to fight continually for better roles. He wanted the title role in *The Jack London Story*, but Warners wouldn't lend him out; nor would they let him do *The Adventures of Martin Eden*. When he asked for the part of George Gershwin in the biographical film, they said he wouldn't look right in a tuxedo. Half-jokingly, half-seriously, Garfield once asked Jack Warner in print, "Parole me!"

Synopsis:

Johnny Blake (John Garfield), misfit and drifter, is hiding from the police, having killed a man in self-defense. He saves the life of Hap O'Connor (Pat O'Brien), an oil-field foreman. The pair later meet as employees of opposing oil companies, and Garfield joins O'Connor. He meets Linda (Frances Farmer), daughter of the eccentric prospector for whom they work. When Hap is injured, Garfield takes over and successfully drills oil. In the climax, he eludes an avalanche to save the burning wells, and he and Linda will be united when he has exonerated himself from the murder charge.

Review:

The New York Times,
September 2, 1940:

Mr. Garfield is still Mr. Garfield which is good enough to make one wish that his producers would cease casting him in the same role film after film. In fact, we don't think Mr. Garfield was running away from a rap at all. He was just a fugitive from Warners.

With Frances Farmer, friend from Group Theatre days

With William Lundigan, Marjorie Rambeau, and Brenda Marshall

EAST OF THE RIVER
1940

Director, Alfred Green; *associate producer*, Harlan Thompson; *script*, Fred Niblo, Jr., from a story by John Fante and Ross B. Willis; *cameraman*, Sid Hickok; *editor*, Thomas Pratt; *released, November 9, 1940; running time*, 73 minutes; Warner Bros.

CAST: John Garfield, Brenda Marshall, Marjorie Rambeau, William Lundigan, George Tobias, Moroni Olsen, Douglas Fowley, Jack LaRue, Jack Carr, Paul Guilfoyle, Russell Hicks, Charlie Foy, Ralph Vollie, Jimmy O'Gatty, Robert Homans, Joe Conti, O'Neill Nolan.

With Brenda Marshall

With Marjorie Rambeau as an Italian mother

89

*With William Lundigan, Marjorie Rambeau, and
Brenda Marshall*

This was a New York–locale production with sets produced on the Warner back lot lacking the skillful design that had been prominent in such productions as *Dead End*. This time Garfield plays a boy of the streets who goes wrong and stays wrong. Unfortunately, the story is overplayed, and Garfield's characterization, done with swagger and a bragging overconfidence, makes him seem more of a Brodway character than a gangster. Coming after the box-office success of *Flowing Gold*, it uses the same characterization—the lovable rogue. Garfield's earlier attempt at natural underplayed comedy and pathos in *Saturday's Children* had been tossed aside, and he was back in a stereotyped mold of the loud, side-of-the-mouth-talking New York crook.

Garfield suffered under this kind of script and direction. He tended to go for a tried and recognizable approach, often clichéd, and to use mannerisms rather than acting to portray his role. The material, of course, demanded little else. One element of his comic ability was briefly exploited in a bizarre (almost out-of-place), zany end sequence, in which he gives up the girl to good brother William Lundigan and outsmarts the crooks who want to kill him by punching a policeman.

Others in the cast, particularly Marjorie Rambeau, delivered purely exaggerated ethnic Italians. Essentially a forgettable film, *East of the River* was an example of studio formula production at its worst.

Synopsis:

Two young street urchins are caught riding the freights and hauled before the police. Joey is the son of an Italian restaurant owner, Mama Raviola, and Nick is an orphan. The mother wins the boys' freedom and adopts Nick, promising to make men of them both.

Years later, at twenty-five, Nick graduates from college and Joey is released from San Quentin (he helped send his adopted brother through school). Joey returns with his moll, Laura (Brenda Marshall), for Nick's graduation.

Eventually Nick falls in love with Laura, and they decide to marry. Joey gets into trouble with the mob and wants Laura to leave town with him on the eve of her engagement to Nick. The mother intervenes and throws Joey out of the house.

The mob shows up at Laura's wedding, but Joey holds them off until Nick and Laura are married.

Review:

The New York Times,
October 8, 1940:

The war of attrition between John Garfield and the law of the realm—or is it just the Warner Brothers?—seems perilously close to its final stages in *East of the River*. . . . Perhaps the uses of Mr. Garfield's talents are nobody's business but his own and Warners, but by the same token it is this corner's business to describe their latest collaboration as contrived and hackneyed. . . . The whole film has the look of a catch-penny attempt to cash in on Mr. Garfield's drawing power at the box office. . . . Isn't it high time that the Warners allowed Mr. Garfield to reform—and stay that way.

With Douglas Fowley and Jack LaRue

Edward G. Robinson as Wolf Larson, Howard da Silva with rope

THE SEA WOLF
1941

Director, Michael Curtiz; *producers*, Jack L. Warner and Hal B. Wallis; *associate producer*, Henry Blanke; *script*, Robert Rossen, from the novel by Jack London; *cameraman*, Sal Polito; *editor*, George Amy; *released, May 22, 1941*; *running time*, 100 minutes; Warner Bros.

CAST: Edward G. Robinson, Alexander Knox, John Garfield, Ida Lupino, Barry Fitzgerald, Gene Lockhart, Stanley Ridges, David Bruce, Francis MacDonald, Howard da Silva, Frank Lacteen.

With Edward G. Robinson and George Magrill

Reunited with Curtiz and working with the top actors at Warners in the supporting cast, Garfield gave one of his most dynamic performances as the rebellious sailor, the enemy of Edward G. Robinson. Admittedly, the strongest performance in the film is Robinson's portrayal of the cruel captain, done with a consummate malevolence, with fine shadings of insights and abrupt changes.

Curtiz, who was the first to see Garfield's potential, was using him for a familiar role—the defiant young man who stands up to corrupt authority. In contrast to Robinson's potent and devilish captain, Garfield's idealist seems weak and ineffectual; Robinson similarly triumphs over the intellectual played by Alexander Knox. Where Garfield's character is weak against the strength of the captain, he is at least able to escape with his ideals; Knox's character, purely rational, is dominated by and destroyed with the captain. Uncannily, all three actors seemed physically to project the strengths and weaknesses of their characters—a hallmark of many Curtiz films.

The Sea Wolf remains exciting and particularly noteworthy for the quality ensemble performance of the cast. Many years later, Edward G. Robinson would note of John Garfield, "John Garfield was one of the best young actors I ever encountered, but his passions about the world were so intense that I feared any day he would have a heart attack. It was not long before he did."

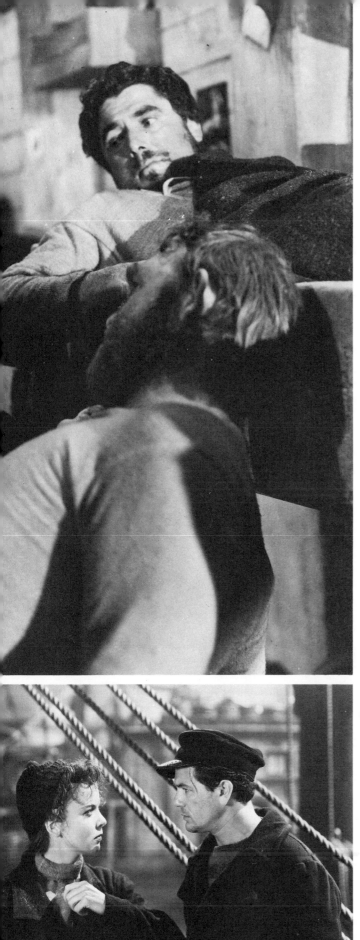

Synopsis:

In a fog-shrouded sea, an accident aboard ship forces Humphrey Van Weyden (Alexander Knox) to take refuge aboard a fishing vessel, the *Ghost*. In the morning, Van Weyden meets the demonic captain of the ship, Wolf Larsen (Edward G. Robinson). The captain refuses to allow Van Weyden to return to shore and insists that he must stay on board as cabin boy, since one of the crew was lost during the storm.

During the voyage, the crew is worked and sweated to the point of mutiny. Led by firebrand rebel George Leech (John Garfield), they revolt but are betrayed, and the leaders are locked below deck by Larsen. In a last desperate effort, the crew does break away and Leech escapes from the ship. The captain, who is losing his sight, tries to hide his infirmity.

The ship is damaged and about to sink, and Van Weyden tries to escape. Van Weyden and Larsen, one wounded and the other blind, are trapped and remain on board as the *Ghost* sinks.

Review:

The New York Times,
March 22, 1941:

When "The Sea Wolf" is topside it rolls along ruthlessly and draws a forbidding picture of oppressive life at sea, of a captain who rules his men without mercy and without heart. . . . John Garfield plays the part of a recalcitrant crewman with concentrated spite.

With Ida Lupino

OUT OF THE FOG
1941

Director, Anatole Litvak; *producer,* Hal B. Wallis; *associate producer,* Henry Blanke; *script,* Robert Rossen, Jerry Wald, and Richard Macauley, from the play *The Gentle People,* by Irwin Shaw; *art director,* Carl Jule Weyl; *musical director,* Leo F. Forbstein; *cameraman,* James Wong Howe; *editor,* Warren Lowe; *special effects,* Rex Wimpy; *released,* June 14, 1941; *running time,* 93 minutes; Warner Bros.

CAST: John Garfield, Ida Lupino, Thomas Mitchell, John Qualen, Eddie Albert, George Tobias, Aline MacMahon, Robert Homans, Bernard Gorcey, Leo Gorcey, Odette Myrtle, Jerome Cowan, Paul Harvey.

Out of the Fog was based on an Irwin Shaw play, originally done on Broadway by the Theatre Guild. Garfield's part was played on stage by Franchot Tone, a fellow Group Theatre member. Garfield was better suited to the role of the cheap, small-time hoodlum who terrorizes the defenseless people of the waterfront community. He acted with a cockiness and self-assurance that revealed the little boy just below the surface. *Out of the Fog* contained the typical elements of the gangster film, but it skillfully arranged them with just enough novel twists to make the drama believable.

The setting is a depressing environment that allows the people who live in it to be the prey of the criminal

With Jimmy Conlin, Alec Craig, Bernard Gorcey, George Tobias, Robert E. Homans, Leo Gorcey, and Odette Myrtle

element. Garfield portrays the criminal, and the victims, two old men, must endure much suffering before they end up on the side of vengeance and justice. One of the striking scenes in the film is when the old men lure Garfield out to sea in their small boat under the pretext of giving him a ride; he has extorted money from them and even taken the young daughter of one of them. Once at sea, the old men have resolved to kill Garfield. They attempt it but fail; then, inadvertently the gangster falls overboard. He cannot swim, and the old men watch as he drowns.

In a final bit of irony he has left his wallet filled with their money on the boat. The old men return and the neighborhood policeman pieces together what happened and simply looks the other way.

In some ways the film was alarming, but in others it was a reaffirmation of the right of the people to defend themselves when the law will not or cannot. Its attitude is defiant and decidedly on the side of moral justice.

In many ways, films such as these went beyond the Hollywood ideal of a simple happy ending. Because of the social orientation the writers gave it, the thrust of the story is for change—the kind of change that would give all the socially disadvantaged a better environment. In a sense, scripts such as these exhibit a fundamental optimism in the ability of men to overcome their environment for the good of all. In other films, where Garfield portrays a victim of the environment, he, too, is able to redeem himself once a door has been opened.

With John Qualen, Eddie Albert, and Thomas Mitchell

With Thomas Mitchell

With Robert E. Homans, Thomas Mitchell, and John Qualen

Synopsis:

Two old men own a small boat in Sheepshead Bay, Brooklyn. They are saving their money to buy a larger one for fishing. One of them, Jonah, must contend with a wife who is a nagging hypochondriac and a daughter who is bitter and resentful of her drab life. Harold Goff (John Garfield), a self-appointed protection racketeer, forces the old men to pay him their savings. On top of that, he entices Jonah's daughter to go away with him, after beating the old man when he threatened to stop them. In desperation, the two old men plan to murder Goff. They entice him aboard their boat but Goff realizes their intent, and in the confusion he falls overboard leaving his wallet with his money on the boat. The old men say nothing of Goff's drowning, and the local policeman, guessing what has happened, looks the other way.

Reviews:

New York Herald Tribune,
June 21, 1941:

It is cheering news . . . that "Out of the Fog" which opened at the Strand yesterday is a work of distinction. . . . [It] is not completely satisfying. The opening sequences are faltering and the concluding episodes are a bit too pat. . . . It follows the original Shaw play "The Gentle People" rather faithfully, but has succeeded in converting a disappointing stage work into a vastly entertaining motion picture.

So far as I can see it is the acting which makes "Out of the Fog" an extraordinary achievement. . . . John Garfield gives what is unquestionably his greatest screen portrayal as the petty hoodlum who turns gentle people into murderers.

The New York Times,
June 21, 1941:

As it is told by the Warners, in their familiar hard-boiled style, it has moments of sinister impact, especially when John Garfield as the gangster is turning on the heat. Mr. Garfield is a sleek and vicious character, a most convincing small time racketeer.

With Esther Dale and Nancy Coleman

DANGEROUSLY THEY LIVE
1941

Director, Robert Florey; *associate producer,* Ben Stoloff; *script,* Marion Parsonnet; *art director,* Hugh Reticher; *cameraman,* L. William O'Connell; *editor,* Harold McLernon; *released, December, 1941; running time,* 77 minutes; Warner Bros.

CAST: John Garfield, Nancy Coleman, Raymond Massey, Moroni Olsen, Lee Patrick, Christian Rub, Roland Drew, Frank Reicher, Esther Dale, John Harmon.

Made prior to the United States's entry into the war, the film was released in December 1941, the month of Pearl Harbor. It relied heavily on growing anti-Nazi feeling and was probably successful despite an improbable and confusing plot. Garfield, departing from his usual role, plays a hospital intern inadvertently helping Nancy Coleman, a beleaguered spy for the good guys. Generally, no one in the film displays any adeptness with his or her part or the confused story. Garfield, out of his milieu in Long Island country

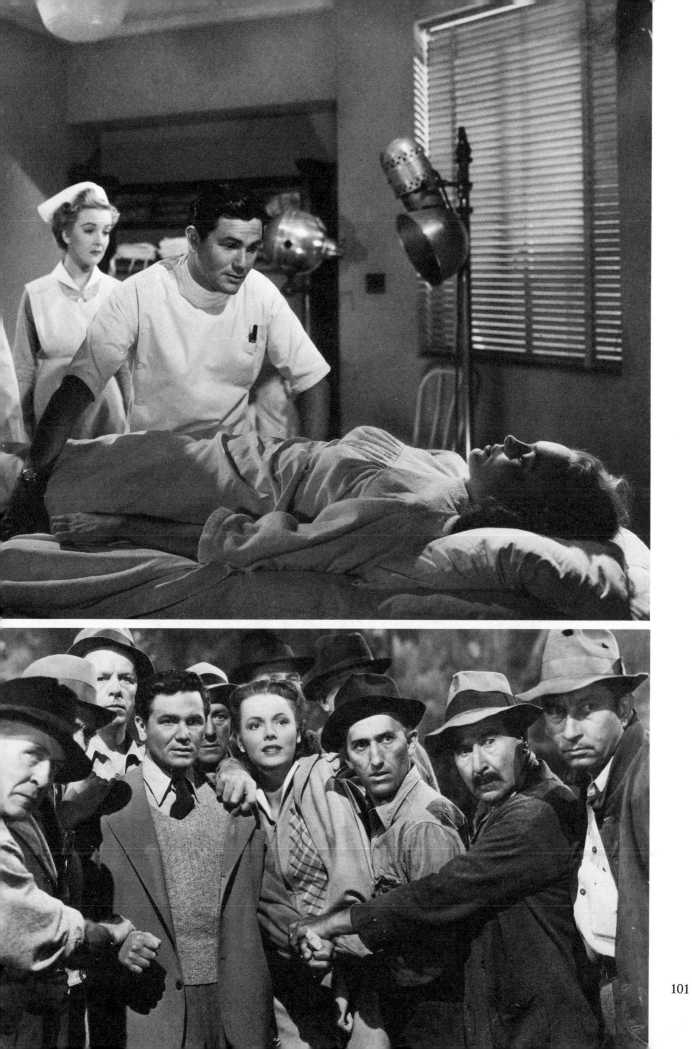

With Nancy Coleman, Raymond Massey and Moroni Olsen.

The police hold Garfield while Raymond Massey looks on.

homes with gardeners and servants, adds to the overall poor performances. The film fed on the general war paranoia of spies, informers, and a growing sense of encroachment from foreigners and foreign ideas. A final confusing sequence of Nazi underground hideaways, knockdown fights, and miraculous rescues does nothing to save this run-of-the-mill film.

Synopsis:

Nancy Coleman is an agent carrying secret information for the Allies and is kidnapped by Nazi agents. In attempting to escape, she is hurt in a traffic accident. Suffering from temporary amnesia, she is taken to a hospital, where John Garfield is an intern assigned to her case. She recovers quickly and tells Garfield of her plight.

A man claiming to be her father arrives with a famous psychiatrist. They take the girl to a country estate and invite Garfield along when he becomes suspicious. At the estate, the two people find themselves virtual prisoners.

Garfield escapes but is thrown into jail when the psychiatrist testifies against him. The girl is taken to a hideout, from which her information will be radioed to a Nazi ship. Garfield escapes from jail and rescues her. The information is then given to an Allied bomber squadron, which intercepts the Nazi submarine in the last sequence.

Review:

The New York Times,
April 11, 1942:

Anyone who has watched a previous Warner pursuit . . . can pretty well call the turns in this not even remotely subtle film. . . . They don't stunt on actors either. John Garfield, the rough-and-ready glamour boy, plays the single-handed hero in this instance with cool and square-jawed conviction.

With Hedy Lar

TORTILLA FLAT
1942

Director, Victor Fleming; *producer*, Sam Zimbalist; *script*, John Lee Mackie and Benjamin Glazer, from the book by John Steinbeck; *art director*, Cedric Gibbons; *music score*, Franz Waxman; *lyrics*, Frank Loesser; *cameraman*, Karl Freund; *editor*, James E. Newcom; *released, April 1942; running time,* 105 minutes; MGM.

CAST: Spencer Tracy, John Garfield, Hedy Lamarr, Frank Morgan, Akim Tamiroff, Sheldon Leonard, John Qualen, Donald Meek, Connie Gilchrist, Allen Jenkins, Henry O'Neill, Mercedes Ruffino, Nina Campana, Arthur Space, Betty Wells, Harry Burns.

As Danny

With Spencer Tracy and Sheldon Leonard

(Below) With Hedy Lamarr, John Qualen, and Sheldon Leonard

106

This, Garfield's first opportunity to work outside the familiar Warner Brothers stable, was with MGM, acknowledged to be the leading studio in Hollywood. He said in print that he enjoyed working at MGM and even hinted that he wouldn't mind doing many more films there, but MGM was ill suited to Garfield's acting abilities. MGM was the renowned purveyor of gloss, the fantasy land of pretty-boy stars and glamorous women. It relied on over-romantic films utilizing Gable and his look-alikes teamed with its many photogenic women actresses. And although no studio in Hollywood professed anything more than profit as its goals, Warner Brothers, for some reason, felt it could make a profit out of the middle and lower classes of American society. It was really the Warners outlook that gave Garfield what little success he was able to glean during his studio years.

Tortilla Flat was a good example of the wrong film for the wrong man. The part lacked the dynamism that Garfield was always able to bring to his acting; also, it required a sustained Spanish accent, which he was never able to bring off. On the whole, the film was a slow and drawn-out version of the Steinbeck novel.

It is interesting that Garfield would get a good acting opportunity at MGM several years later, with *The Postman Always Rings Twice.*

Synopsis:

The adventures of Danny (John Garfield) and Pilon (Spencer Tracy) and their friends, the paisanos of a small fishing village. Danny's inheritance of two houses brings him instant respectability and estranges him from Pilon and his other friends. Danny and Pilon vie for the affection of Dolores and become near enemies. But when one of Danny's houses burns down and Danny is hurt in a fight, Pilon comes to his aid, and all ends happily.

Review:

The New York Times,
May 22, 1942:

With Spencer Tracy, John Garfield, Akim Tamiroff and a batch of raffish . . . lusty paisanos—the work-shirking, wine-guzzling heroes of the tale—it emerges as a winning motion picture and a deterrent to respectable enterprise. . . . And all of the actors—yes all of them—have delineated robust characters. Mr. Tracy, the roguish Pilone, is splendid in this earthy role. Mr. Garfield is a lovable, lively Danny.

As Sgt. Winocki

AIR FORCE
1943

Director, Howard Hawkes; *producer*, Hal B. Wallis; *script*, Dudley Nichols; *aerial photography*, Elmer Syer and Charles Marshall; *special effects*, Roy Davidson and Rex Wimpy; *art director,* John Huglies; *musical score*, Franz Waxman; *music director*, Leo F. Forbstein; *cameraman*, James Wong Howe; *editor*, George Amy; *released, March 20, 1943; running time*, 124 minutes; Warner Bros.

CAST: John Garfield, John Ridgely, Gig Young, Harry Carey, George Tobias, Charles Drake, Arthur Kennedy.

This was Garfield's only film under director Howard Hawkes, and while it was a small role, it was considered part of the Hollywood wartime effort. The hero of the film is a Boeing B-17 bomber, and the action takes place during the first weeks of the Japanese invasion.

Garfield's part, like most of the character roles in the film, was a straight stereotype—his familiar one of the tough kid who defies authority but in the end comes through for his country and his mates. His performance is generally undistinguished but accurate within the

With Ward Wood, Ray Montgomery, Harry Carey, and George Tobias

premise of the story. Actually, the film is famous for a deathbed scene, written by William Faulkner, in which a dying commander, with his crew beside him, flies his ship for the last time.

In a way, films such as these were a donation on the part of top actors such as Garfield—with a small part and little scope for performance, they were seen as giving wartime service.

Synopsis:

Aboard the *Mary Ann* fighter bomber, bound for Honolulu, December 6, 1941, the crew discovers that Hickok field is off the air. They are forced to make an emergency landing, only to take off when they are attacked by the Japanese. After several mishaps, they are told to proceed to Australia, dropping bombs on Japanese ships along the way.

Their plane is damaged and the commander wounded. The crew is ordered to bail out, and Garfield brings the ship down with the wounded pilot aboard. The ship is patched up and used for action in the Coral Sea. Finally, hit and damaged, the *Mary Ann* lands on an Australian beach.

Reviews:

New York Daily News,
February 1943:

The story . . . is simply told on the screen by Dudley Nichols, who wrote a powerfully effective screen play; by Howard Hawks, whose masterly direction of the picture makes it an outstanding achievement, and a male cast that is distinguished by the excellence of its team work.

John Garfield heads the cast, but he is no more important to the picture than any other actor who represents a member of the crew.

The New York Times,
February 4, 1943:

Mr. Hawkes very wisely recruited a cast with no outstanding star, thus assuring himself the privilege of giving every one a chance. . . . John Garfield's tough creation of Winoki is superior despite its brevity.

With Joy Barlow

DESTINATION TOKYO
1943

Director, Delmer Daves; *producer*, Jerry Wald; *musical score*, Franz Waxman; *art director*, Leo K. Kuter; *music director*, Leo F. Forbstein; *script*, Delmer Daves and Albert Maltz, from a story by Steve Fisher; *cameraman*, Bert Glennon; *special effects*, Laurence Butler and Willard Van Enger; *editor*, Charles Nyby; *released, May 25, 1943; running time,* 135 minutes; Warner Bros.

CAST: Cary Grant, John Garfield, Alan Hale, John Ridgely, Dane Clark, Warner Anderson, William Prince, Robert Hutton, Peter Whitney, Faye Emerson, Warren Douglas, John Forsythe, John Alvin, Bill Kennedy, William Challe, Whit Bissell, Stephen Richards, John Whitney, George Lloyd, Tom Tully, Maurice Murphy.

With Cary Grant, John Forsythe, Alan Hale, and Peter Whitney, Tom Tully and Robert Hutton

This wartime film gave some glimpse into the real-life situation of a submarine crew on combat duty. Unfortunately, the film is too long, and the action footage has been seen so often since then that it is no longer novel or interesting. What is interesting is the type casting of the two stars, Garfield and Grant; Grant obviously looks and talks like an officer, a respectable man with a wife and family, while Garfield with his accent and rough looks, is a common girl-chasing sailor. This is also the first appearance of Dane Clark in a film with Garfield. Newcomer Clark seems to have modeled himself closely on the Garfield style. Because he didn't have Garfield's range of ability, he brings out the worst techniques of the style—he is loud and too intense, with a tendency to overplay the emotion in a scene. Next to him, Garfield tones down, instinctively pulling back his character and gaining something by doing it.

Synopsis:

Acting under sealed orders, Cary Grant, as

submarine commander, takes his sub to sea and heads for the Aleutians. Here he picks up an air-corps officer. The orders detail a reconnaissance patrol off Tokyo Bay to obtain information useful in making air raids on Japan. The air-corps officer and Wolf (John Garfield) are landed when the sub maneuvers into the bay. They obtain the information and it is radioed to a U.S. aircraft carrier, and soon a formation of bombers embarks to attack Tokyo.

Review:

The New York Times,
January 1, 1944:

[Destination Tokyo] is a studiously purposeful "epic" of the submarine service in this war. . . . There is John Garfield as a torpedoman with a great line of gab about "dames."

With Maureen O'Hara

THE FALLEN SPARROW
1943

Director, Richard Wallace; *producer*, Robert Fellows; *musical score*, Roy Webb; *music director*, C. Bakalenkoff; *art directors*, Albert D'Agostino and Mark Lee Kirk; *cameraman*, Nicholas Musuraca; *special effects*, Vernon Y. Walker; *editor*, Robert Wise; *script*, Warren Duff, from the novel by Dorothy B. Hughes; *released, August 1943; running time, 94 minutes;* RKO.

CAST: John Garfield, Maureen O'Hara, Patricia Morison, Martha O'Driscoll, John Miljan, Walter Slezak, Hugh Beaumont, Bruce Edwards, John Banner, Sam Goldberg.

With John Miljan

Garfield's role as a former fighter in the Lincoln Brigade from the Spanish civil war showed that Hollywood was at least trying to confront real issues. Unfortunately, the script fails because it will not tackle the subject entirely; it circles around the issues and is afraid to come out and say what it is about. Because of the clash between communists and fascists in Spain, the subject was heady material even during the war against Germany and Italy—but the script just won't name the names.

The director was content to focus the camera on the brooding face of Garfield and let him suggest the inner turmoil of the character. Moreover, Maureen O'Hara seems totally miscast in this grim world of former agents, spies, and society decadents, while Walter Slezak is diabolical as a cross between Peter Lorre and Sidney Greenstreet. Garfield must have been sympathetic to the politics of the film, but it is next to impossible to make a coherent statement of what the hero's politics are—he won't say. The facts, it must have been concluded, were still too difficult for an American audience to take. It would be left to the French to do it many years later in *La Guerre Est Finie*.

With Martha O'Driscoll

Synopsis:

Garfield is a returned Spanish civil war veteran who had been tortured in a fascist prison camp. He has managed to send home a battle souvenir, a flag from one of Hitler's personal regiments. The friend who received the flag has mysteriously committed suicide, and Garfield is constantly watched by foreign agents.

He meets a beautiful aristocrat (Maureen O'Hara), who has been forced to lead Garfield into a trap set by the German agent (Walter Slezak). The agent practices a kind of mental torture on the veteran, calling upon the worst days of his prison confinement.

On the brink of capitulating, Garfield is held prisoner in a house full of German agents. But he manages to withstand the mental punishment and break out, rescuing Maureen O'Hara at the same time.

Review:

The New York Times,
August 20, 1943:

Out of a bizarre idea RKO has produced a strange and restless melodrama. . . . By virtue of a taut performance by John Garfield in the title role, and the singular skill with which director Richard Wallace has highlighted the significant climaxes, "The Fallen Sparrow" is one of the uncommon and provocatively handled melodramas of recent months. . . . Mr. Garfield remains almost constantly convincing and without his sure and responsive performance in a difficult role, Mr. Wallace's efforts would have been lost entirely.

THANK YOUR LUCKY STARS
1943

Director, David Butler; *producer*, Mark Hellinger; *script*, Melvin Frank, James V. Kern, and Norman Panama, from a story by Everett Freeman and Arthur Schwartz; *dance director*, Leroy Prinz; *art director*, Anton Grot and Leo K. Kuter; *songs*, Arthur Schwartz and Frank Loesser; *camera*, Arthur Edeson and Irene Moore; *released, September 25, 1943; running time,* 127 minutes; Warner Bros.

CAST: Eddie Cantor, Bette Davis, John Garfield, Alan Hale, Dennis Morgan, Jack Carson, Joan Leslie, Ida Lupino, S. Z. Sakall, Alexis Smith, Humphrey Bogart, Olivia de Havilland, Errol Flynn, Ann Sheridan, Dinah Shore, George Tobias, Edward Everett Horton, Hattie McDaniel, Ruth Donnelly, Don Wilson, Willie Best, Henry Armetta, Joyce Reynolds, Spike Jones and his City Slickers.

Thank Your Lucky Stars must rank among the worst films ever made. At its best, it is two hours of third-rate vaudeville. Actually, Garfield's part was a brief stint giving a tough-guy rendition of "Blues in the Night"—a thoroughly forgettable version. The approach was fairly common at all the studios—pack all the contract players in a loosely devised vaudeville plot and let them be cute. As a second-billed feature, it was supposed to attract people into the movie theaters on the basis of the star-packed cast list. All the studios tried to capitalize on this type of film, and during the war they became briefly popular with such versions as *Stage Door Canteen* and *Hollywood Canteen*.

Synopsis:

A loosely constructed plot revolves around Eddie Cantor's efforts to dominate a benefit performance starring the Warners' repertory of stars and Dennis Morgan's efforts to become a part of the show.

Review:

The New York Times,
October 2, 1943:

It does seem that Warner Brothers could have thought of a better device for getting their stars before the camera to do their acts. . . . But, John Garfield is highly amusing singing a tough guy's version of "Blues in the Night." . . .

With Robert Hutton and Ken Dibbs

HOLLYWOOD CANTEEN
1943

Director, Delmer Daves; *producer,* Walter Gottlieb; *script,* Delmer Daves; *music,* Leroy Prinz; *art director,* Leo K. Kuter; *music director,* Leo F. Forbstein; *cameraman,* Bert Glennon; *editor,* Christian Nyby; *released, December 5, 1943; running time,* 124 minutes, Warner Bros.

CAST: Andrews Sisters, Jack Benny, Joe E. Brown, Eddie Cantor, Kitty Carlisle, Jack Carson, Dane Clark, Joan Crawford, Helmut Dantine, Bette Davis, Faye Emerson, John Garfield, Paul Henreid, Robert Hutton, Andrea King, Joan Leslie, Peter Lorre, Ida Lupino, Irene Manning, Nora Martin, Joan McCracken, Dolores Moran, Dennis Morgan, Janis Paige, Eleanor Parker, William Prince, Joyce Reynolds, John Ridgely, Roy Rogers, S. Z. Sakall, Zachary Scott, Alexis Smith, Barbara Stanwyck, Craig Stevens, Joseph Szigeti, Donald Woods, Jane Wyman, Jimmy Dorsey's orchestra, Carman Cavallaro's orchestra, Golden Gates quartet, Rosario and Antonio, Sons of the Pioneers, Mary Gordon, Betty Brodel, Eddie Marr, Robert Shayne.

Hollywood Canteen is among the more famous of the wartime morale boosters. Its plot is so grotesquely fictitious that it helps to rank the film as "high camp" today. Based on the same idea as *Thank Your Lucky Stars*, it was helped by the general wartime spirit and was fairly successful at the box office. Garfield's role was really behind the scenes; he appeared on screen as one of the famous star waiters taking care of our boys in uniform, but he was actually one of the organizers of the real Hollywood Canteen. He and Bette Davis had raised funds and people for a Hollywood version of the USO club. The film was thus an effort by Warner Brothers both to capitalize on the idea and to help it along.

One interesting note on the film is that it was written and directed by Delmer Daves, who later would be associated with more important films. Daves also wrote the script for *Stage Door Canteen*, a similar star-studded extravaganza, this time set in New York City's USO center. Although just as sentimental as *Hollywood Canteen*, the New York version has a certain warmth and genuineness about it that are totally lacking in the other.

Synopsis:

Robert Hutton as a lonely young GI wanders into the Hollywood Canteen in search of a glimpse of his dream woman, Joan Leslie. All the famous stars of the Warners lot then conspire to have the young soldier meet Miss Leslie. In the interim several of them perform short bits for the huge soldier audience.

Review:

The New York Times,
December 16, 1943:

If it's quality you want in your entertainment and just a slight touch of dramatic grace, beware the elaborate "hocus pocus" of "Hollywood Canteen." . . . To be perfectly blunt about it, this film seems a most distasteful show of Hollywood's sense of its importance.

With Zachary Scott, Johnny Mitchell, Julie Bishop, Joyce Reynolds, Fay Emerson, Andrea King, Eleanor Parker, Dolores Moran, Lynn Baggott,
Bette Davis, John Ridgeley, Robert Hutton, and Joan Leslie

Edmund Gwenn, Fay Emerson, Gilbert Emery, Isobel Elsom, George Tobias, Dennis King, Sara Allgood, and George Coulouris

With Dennis King and Sidney Greenstreet

With Faye Emerson

BETWEEN TWO WORLDS
1944

Director, Edward A. Blatt; *producer*, Mark Hellinger; *script*, Daniel Fuchs, based on the play *Outward Bound*, by Sutter Vane; *cameraman*, Carl Guthrie; *editor*, Rudi Fehr; *released, October 1944; running time*, 74 minutes; Warner Bros.

CAST: John Garfield, Paul Henreid, Sydney Greenstreet, Eleanor Parker, Edmund Gwenn, George Tobias, George Coulouris, Faye Emerson, Sara Algood, Dennis King, Isobel Elsom, Gilbert Emery, Lester Matthews, Pat O'Moore.

This was the second film of the play *Outward Bound* (the first had starred Leslie Howard). At the time, it must have seemed particularly suited to the wartime mood. The story of a death ship and its passengers bound for the other world relied mainly on its eerie mood and atmosphere for effect. In this version the mood is sacrificed to realism, effectively undermining the potential of the script. Garfield, too, seemed out of place in the film; his role, of a hard-bitten newspaper reporter who has seen and done everything and cares for nothing, just doesn't fit him.

At thirty-one, Garfield projected a chip-on-the-shoulder combativeness suited to a young man on the way up, not down. His performance is all in one key—the strutting and brashness he always fell back on when the part or the director offered him little else. Because of the effort toward realism, the subtlety of the script was gone, and most of the other actors also relied on stereotyped performances.

At the very end Garfield makes a confession of his debased and useless life and asks, "Where did I go wrong?" A good question for the director.

Synopsis:

During a World War II air raid a bomb demolishes a car filled with passengers bound for a transatlantic liner leaving an English port. A former Austrian pianist and his wife are hurled to the ground by the blast. Later, despondent, the young couple form a pact to commit suicide in their apartment by turning on the gas. They suddenly find themselves aboard a fog-shrouded vessel. When they recognize the passengers as those who were in the car struck by the bomb, they realize it is a death ship.

The wise-cracking newspaperman (John Garfield) is the first of the passengers to guess that they are all dead. The others will not accept it until the Examiner (Sidney Greenstreet) appears. He is to decide their fates according to the lives they led on earth. The suicides cannot leave the ship but must travel between life and death—but the Examiner gives them another chance, and they wake in their apartment as the gas fumes are swept away through a bomb-shattered window.

Review:

The New York Times,
May 6, 1944:

This production is competent, though the script runs entirely to discourse and Director Edward Blatt has managed to move his people around with some pain. . . . John Garfield is somewhat too splashy as the brokendown newspaperman, and his popular talent for "tough" roles makes his casting in this dubious.

Telling George Coulouris, Isobel Elsom, Sara Allgood, Paul Henried and Eleanor Parker that they are dead

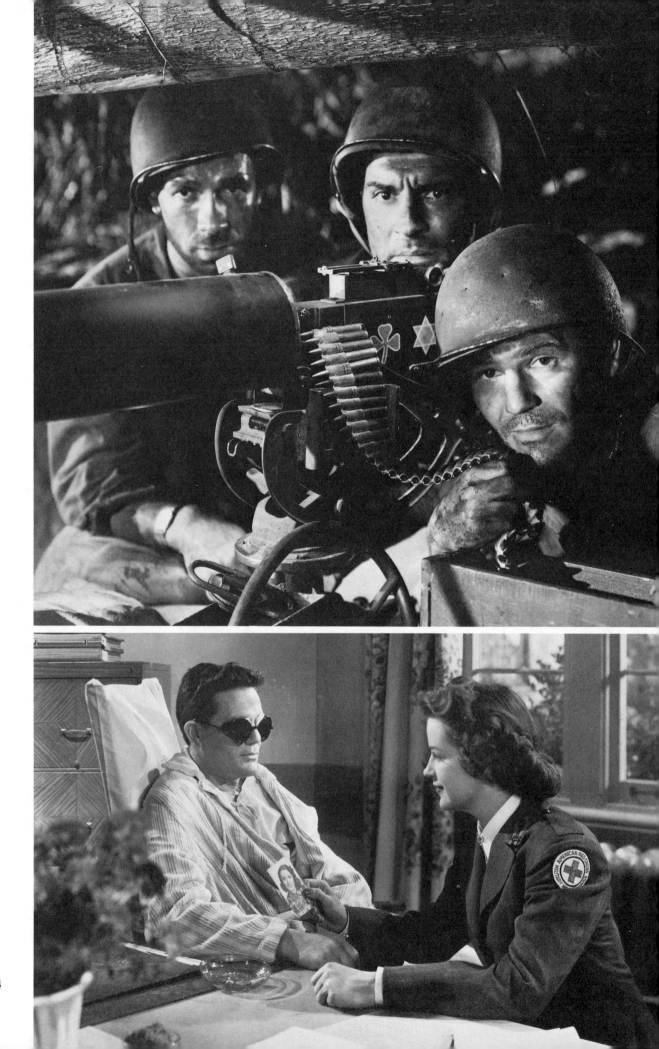

With Dane Clark and Anthony Caruso

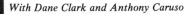

With Eleanor Parker

PRIDE OF THE MARINES
1945

Director, Delmer Daves; *producer*, Jerry Wald; *script*, Albert Maltz, from a story by Roger Butterfield; *adaptation*, Marvin Borowsky; *musical score*, Franz Waxman; *art director*, Leo K. Kuter; *music director*, Leo F. Forbstein; *special effects*, L. Robert Burgs; *cameraman*, Peverell Marley; *editor*, Owen Marks; *released, September 1, 1945; running time,* 119 minutes; Warner Bros.

CAST: John Garfield, Dane Clark, Eleanor Parker, John Ridgely, Rosemary De Camp, Ann Doran, Ann Todd, Warren Douglas, Don McGuire, Tom D'Andrea, Rory Mallinson, Stephen Richards, Anthony Caruso, Moroni Olsen, Dave Willock, John Sheridan, John Miles, John Campton, Lennie Bremen, Michael Brown.

As blinded soldier Al Schmid, with Rosemary De Camp

The role of Al Schmid, as played by Garfield, was a triumph of his style of acting. His sense of realism and his ability to infuse a role with life and understanding had finally come together in this film. An intelligent script helped enormously. It was a portrayal of one of the many heroes who served during the war. Garfield was able to bring to life this average man from a working-class origin, to show his modest and simple goals and discoveries without making them maudlin. The script was also enhanced by a very straightforward love affair marked more by its ease than by its passion.

In all this Garfield was playing a part made for him, one to which he could bring all he had learned and put it to good use. He no longer needed to shout or lash out in a frenzy—all this he left to Dane Clark, who played his friend. The contrast, between a man eager and enthusiastic for life in the early sequences and a man who has been immobilized in the later part, is still gripping. Garfield could play a blind man toppling over a Christmas tree, and the rage was in his helplessness. This was combined with some excellent battle sequences, some of the most realistic that had ever appeared in a fictional film.

Only two scenes seem out of place today. One was a special-effects scene, shot in negative, in which Garfield as Schmid fantasizes about his blindness and rejection

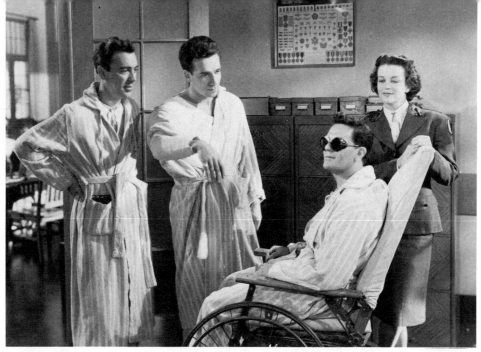

With Rosemary De Camp, Dane Clark and Tom D'Andrea

With Mark Stevens, Warren Douglas, Rosemary DeCamp, and Dane Clark

With Dane Clark

by his friends. The effect was obvious and unnecessary. The other was an overoptimistic and patriotic sequence in a hospital for wounded veterans. Patriotism, when spoken directly at the audience, somehow does not wear well on screen.

Synopsis:

This is the true story of Al Schmid and his wife, Ruth Hartley. Al, a Philadelphia workingman, is thrust into the war in 1941. He is little concerned with politics, sharing his work and hobbies with his girlfriend, Ruth, and the family he lives with, the Merchants.

Al is a member of a machine-gun crew on Guadalcanal defending a salient against a Japanese attack. The two men with him are wounded, and Al must defend the position though blinded by a grenade blast. He succeeds but has lost his sight.

At a San Diego hospital he is told that the medical treatment on his eyes has failed. He is ordered to return home. Bitter and disappointed, he does not want to be with Ruth or any of his friends, even though it is Christmas. Finally, after holding his emotions in, Al seeks the comfort of his friends. He is decorated for his heroism and is once again eager for life, though resigned to his handicap.

Reviews:

The New York Times,
August 25, 1945:

A remarkably natural production . . . gives the story integrity. . . . Albert Maltz took the journalistic accounts of Schmid's experience and translated them into a solid, credible drama, composed of taut situation and dialogue. . . . John Garfield does a brilliant job as Schmid, cocky, and self-reliant and full of a calm, commanding pride.

New York Herald Tribune,
August 25, 1945:

Honesty and intensity make up for numerous cinematic faults in "Pride of the Marines." . . . Thanks to John Garfield's brilliant portrayal of the central role, Schmid emerges on the screen with genuine personal authority. . . . Garfield's underacting keys the production to its central theme.

With Eleanor Parker

THE POSTMAN ALWAYS RINGS TWICE
1946

Director, Tay Garnett; *producer*, Carey Wilson; *script*, Harry Rusking and Niven Busch, based on the novel by James M. Cain; *art directors*, Cedric Gibbons and Randall Duell; *musical score*, George Busserman; *cameraman*, Sidney Wagner; *editor*, George White; *released*, *May 1946*; *running time*, 113 minutes; MGM.

CAST: John Garfield, Lana Turner, Cecil Kellaway, Hume Cronyn, Leon Ames, Audrey Totter, Alan Reed, Jeff York.

With Lana Turner and Cecil Kellaway

With Lana Turner

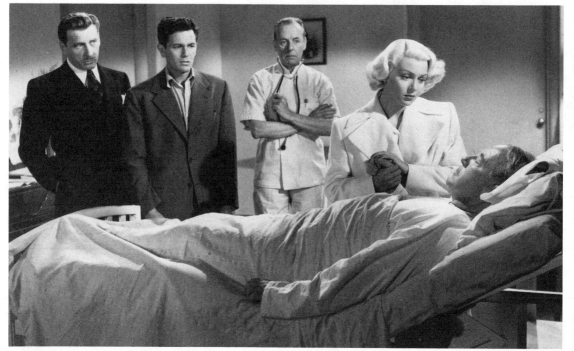

With Leon Ames, Edward Earl, Miss Turner, and Cecil Kellaway

Planning the murder

Postman is more interesting for the visual and physical tension between Lana Turner and John Garfield than for any other single element. Much of the credit for this is due to the director, Tay Garnett, who kept Lana Turner's hair bleached platinum blond for the part. Her clothes were either stark white or completely black, and Turner's eerie whiteness was quite effective when contrasted to Garfield's dark, brooding features. On screen, Turner and Garfield produced a kind of electricity, a repressed tone of sexuality that carried much of the mood of the picture. Under Garnett's direction, they were probably the most interesting male-female combination on film that year.

The James M. Cain story is steeped in repressed sexuality, involving a bizarre love triangle among the two young lovers and an elderly husband played by Cecil Kelleway, who smiles maniacally even when he is being murdered. Several scenes stand out both visually and dramatically, particularly the murder sequence in which they try to electrocute the old man. Another visually arresting sequence is the first meeting between Garfield and Turner, she dressed in a white suit with short pants. The cynicism they display in the courtroom, and excellent portrayals by Hume Cronyn and Leon Ames as mercenary lawyers, provide a good twist. But somehow, much of the dialogue fails to match the

133

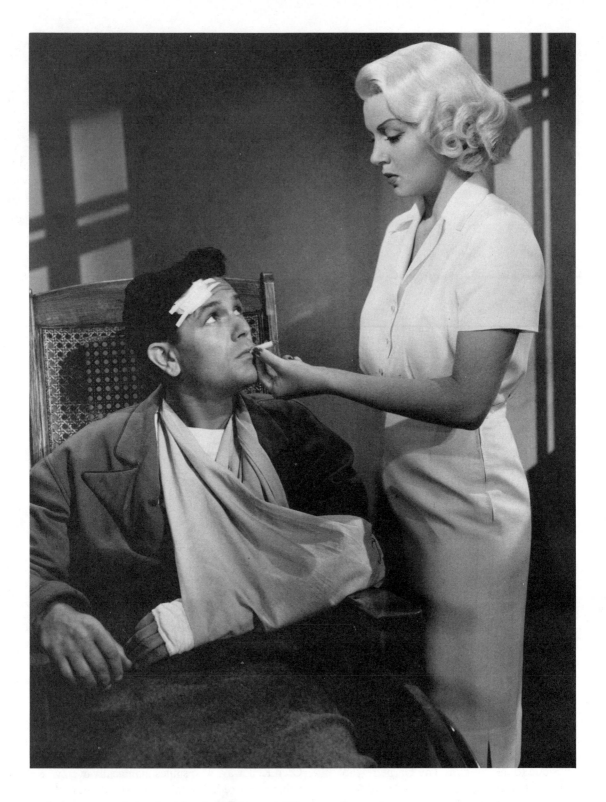

performances and mood set by the two actors. What was needed was the kind of hard-boiled language treatment that had distinguished such films as *The Big Sleep* and *The Maltese Falcon*.

For Garfield, this was only his second film outside Warners in seven years. Despite the mediocre script, *Postman* was a huge success and an important step in Lana Turner's career.

Synopsis:

Lana Turner plays the frustrated, power-hungry young wife of elderly Cecil Kelleway. She has married the older man as a way of getting out of poverty and social insignificance. Into their life comes a young man (John Garfield), a vagabond with vague notions of seeing the world and having new experiences.

With Leon Ames

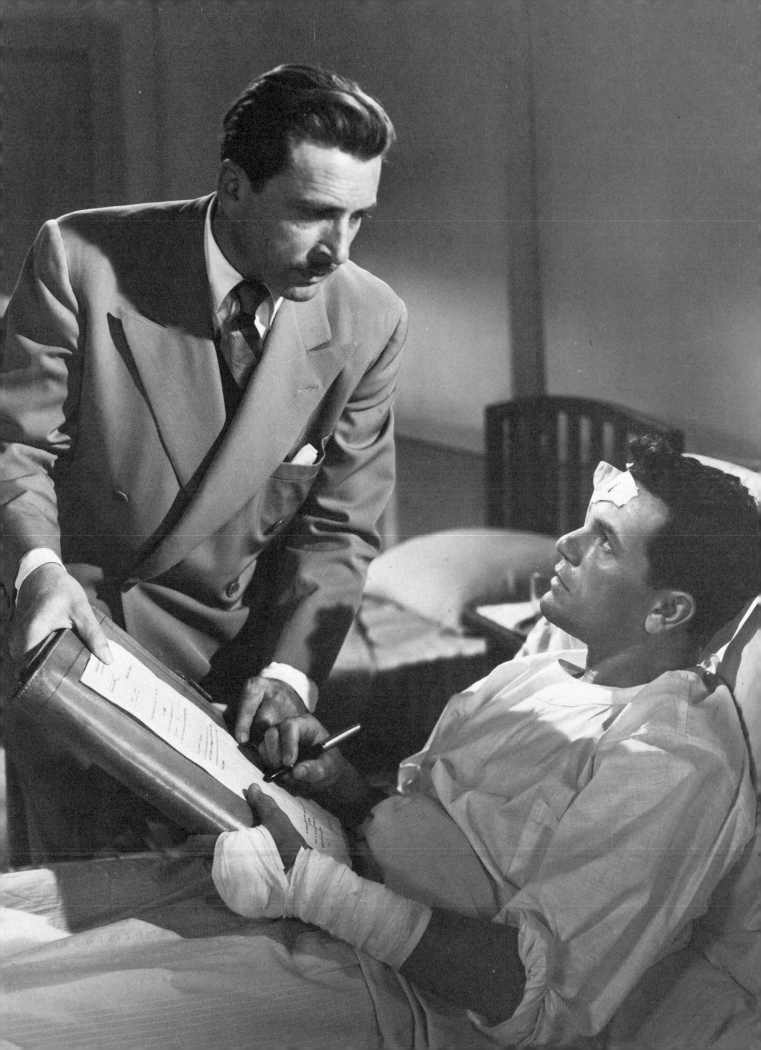

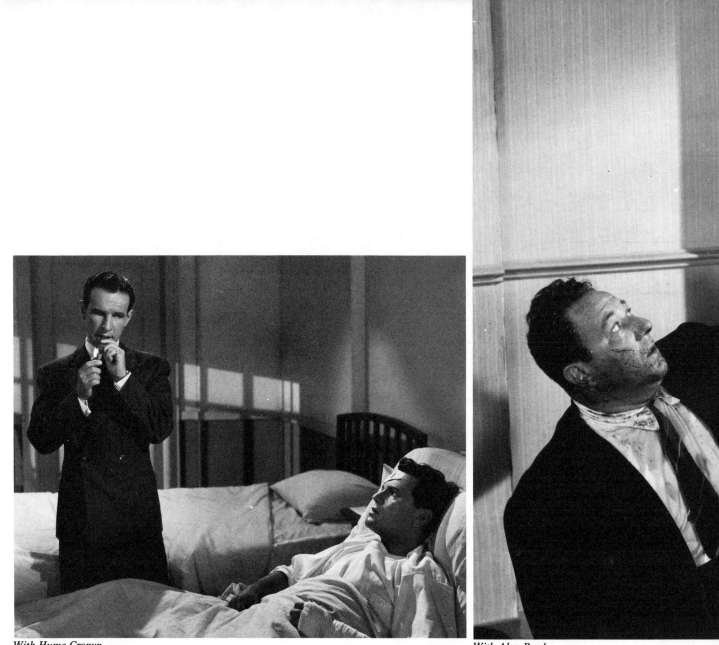

With Hume Cronyn

With Alan Reed

The young people are fatally attracted in spite of their constant bickering. Eventually they plan the murder of the husband. Their first attempt is a failure, and the husband survives, demonically watching the lovers squirm in his presence. Their love seems to grow into hatred, but they are unable to stop, and they finally succeed in killing the old man.

Instantly, their love is dissipated, and when they are discovered, each is coaxed to implicate the other in the crime.

Reviews:

New York Herald Tribune,
May 3, 1946:

James M. Cain's tough story about lust and murder has lost some of its sting in "The Postman Always Rings Twice." The actors pull no punches. But like so many of its companion pieces the film compromises just a bit too much. The ending is chiefly to blame for this predicament. . . . Since the resolution of violence is fabricated in a completely different idiom from the essential melodrama it is an unfortunate letdown. . . .

Mr. Garfield does the major work in keeping the production a savage account of murder for profit. He is excellent as a stumble-bum mechanic who moves into a roadside stand . . . and steals the proprietor's wife, while conspiring with her on matricide. He plays with sullen emphasis.

The New York Times,
May 3, 1946:

The picture achieves its distinction through the smart way in which it has been made and through the quality of its representation of the passion-torn characters. . . . Too much cannot be said for the principals. Mr. Garfield reflects the life of the crude and confused young hobo who stumbles aimlessly into a fatal trap. . . . In its surface aspects, "The Postman" appears no more than a melodramatic tale. . . . But the artistry of writer and actors have made it much more than that; it is, indeed, a sincere comprehension of an American tragedy.

With Geraldine Fitzgerald

With Walter Brennan, seated, and George Tobias

NOBODY LIVES FOREVER
1946

Director, Jean Negulesco; *producer*, Robert Buckner; *script*, W. R. Burnett; *music arrangements*, Jerome Moross; *music director*, Leo F. Forbstein; *art director*, Hugh Reticker; *cameraman*, Arthur Edeson; *special effects*, William McGann and W. Van Enger; *editor*, Rudi Fehr; *released, October 12, 1946; running time,* 100 minutes; Warner Bros.

CAST: John Garfield, Geraldine Fitzgerald, Faye Emerson, George Coulouris, George Tobias, Walter Brennan, Robert Shayne, Richard Gaines, Dick Erdman, James Flavin, Ralph Peters, Alex Havler, William Edmunds, Ralph Dunn, Grady Sutton.

This was one of several films in which Garfield acted for director Jean Negulesco. Essentially, Negulesco worked to create atmosphere, rather than story movement and action. Although Garfield was able to give some of his best restrained performances under Negulesco's direction, he needed a moving story line to keep pace with.

The film starts out as a New York story, then shifts abruptly to the West Coast. The scene change works well in establishing the two sides of the Garfield screen character—the hard-bitten former con man, changed by his war experiences, now groping for a new life. Flamboyant New York night scenes are contrasted with walks on the Pacific beach and scenes of open air and beautiful Los Angeles.

Since the film works hard to create a mood, rather than forcing the action, Garfield gets a chance to convey his emotional turmoil without punching someone in the nose. The sense of boiling emotion under the surface, the need to control what is seething inside him, makes the character interesting and the tedious plot bearable. But it is impossible to keep action out of a Garfield film, and there is a suitable shootout at the end, a waterfront sequence done in hazy fog, again more interesting for mood and effect than for the action. Also handled well are scenes of high-class West Coast life with Garfield appearing as a diamond in the rough, a man at ease in any surroundings but definitely out of place all the time.

Synopsis:

Nick Blake (John Garfield), former con man, returns from the war, to find that his girlfriend has taken his money and found another man. Disillusioned, he leaves New York and heads west to California with his friend Al. There, Nick is induced to swindle a charming, lonely widow out of her fortune. He does not like the assorted thieves and con men involved in the deal but goes ahead with the plan. Nick falls in love with the widow and decides to make a clean break, paying the others off with his own money. When the widow is kidnapped by Nick's accomplices, he rescues her and redeems himself.

Review:

The New York Times,
November 2, 1946:

[The film follows] a formula which has been generally successful in the past. . . . In the roles of [hero and heroine] John Garfield and Geraldine Fitzgerald turn in acting roles which are worthy of better material.

With Geraldine Fitzgerald

HUMORESQUE
1946

Director, Jean Negulesco; *producer,* Jerry Wald; *script,* Clifford Odets and Zachary Gold, from the book by Fannie Hurst; *cameraman,* Ernest Haller; *music director,* Leo F. Forbstein; *art director,* Hugh Reticher; *editor,* Rudi Fehr; *released, December 1946; running time,* 125 minutes; Warner Bros.

Cast: John Garfield, Joan Crawford, Oscar Levant, J. Carrol Naish, Joan Chandler, Tom D'Andrea, Peggy Knudsen, Ruth Nelson, Craig Stevens, Paul Cavanagh, Richard Gaines, John Abbott, Peg LaCentura, Richard Walsh.

With Joan Chandler, Oscar Levant, and Joan Crawford

Written in part by Clifford Odets, the script has almost humorous resemblances to his *Golden Boy,* but this time the poor boy from the ghetto does become a violinist. Garfield, with Oscar Levant as his wise-cracking friend, fiddles his way to the top of the social ladder. He is taken in by wealthy heiress Joan Crawford. If Turner and Garfield were an explosive combination, Crawford and Garfield were the reverse. It was impossible to believe in them as a romantic pair.

The overartful suicide scene, in which Joan Crawford walks into the ocean when she finds out that Garfield loves his violin more than her, is too absurd to be believed.

One of the interesting elements concerned the music (Isaac Stern's playing was dubbed). Garfield's violin playing was faked in contortionist style, with hands tucked through his coat as if he were an amusement-park cardboard cutout. Negulesco

explained: "We made a big hole in the elbow of John Garfield's coat, and a real violinist's hand came through it and fingered the violin. Another violinist was behind him—there were three guys—doing the bowing, and John Garfield was in the middle." The effect was so convincing that Garfield was often requested to play the violin when he appeared on publicity tours for the film.

In a sense the film was a marriage of two styles that did not go together—Negulesco's reliance on mood and atmosphere and Garfield's essentially intense, realistic acting were antithetical. In their three films together this incompatibility is always obvious. *Humoresque* in many ways exhibits all the triteness and clichés of the screen character Garfield had portrayed during his Warners years. As his last film for the company, it is a sad reminder that Warners was never interested in the quality of their films, but only in the profits. There, as at the other studios, quality always depended on the

hired help. When *Humoresque* was successful, Warners was ready to offer a lucrative new contract to Garfield, one they were sure he would accept.

Synopsis

Paul Boray (John Garfield), a young violinist from the wrong side of the tracks, becomes enamored of wealthy dilettante Helen Wright (Joan Crawford). She soon becomes his patron and lover. Helen is used to having her way and ruling everyone around her. She is baffled by Boray, a dedicated artist who puts his music above all else.

Boray's lower-class family disapproves of his relationship with Helen. Though they often quarrel, the two are drawn together magnetically. Eventually, Boray feels he must choose between his music and Helen. They have quarreled again, and Boray is playing Wagner's "Liebestod" at a concert. Helen listens to his music on the radio at home. Unable to reconcile herself to Boray's life and goals, she commits suicide by walking into the nearby ocean.

Review:

The New York Times,
December 26, 1946:

The Warner Brothers have wrapped this piteous affair in a blanket of soul-tearing music which is supposed to make it spiritually purgative. . . . Joan Crawford wobbles out soused to the ears and having to cast herself tragically into the sea after a telephone conversation with John Garfield, who has told her that he loves his fiddle more. . . .

INDEPENDENT FILMS

After his Warners contract expired, Garfield was one of several former studio workers who became independent producers of their own films. Garfield set up shop under the Enterprise Productions banner, an interesting and fairly original operation of independent workers—directors, writers, technicians, and actors. Enterprise was more than an outlet for financial independence; it was a grouping of people with a shared though sometimes varied political point of view. They were committed both to box office profits and to dealing with socially important themes in their films. Although neither goal was often fully realized, the venture probably marked the first time such a group of working artists in Hollywood assembled together.

Robert Aldrich, the director, was involved in several Enterprise projects, including *Body and Soul*. He explained, "While Enterprise did have an orientation toward stories with 'social significance,' I think it would be unfair to say that that was its 'aim.' As the Irish say, this was just before the troubles, and the talented people in that period—there were always exceptions, of course —tended to be more liberal than the untalented people, and because they were more liberal, they got caught up in social processes that had political manifestations which later proved to be economically difficult to live with. In its search for talented and interesting people Enterprise hired a great many followers of that persuasion, and its pictures consequently began to acquire more and more social content."

In the long run, very little actual political propagandizing went on in the films; instead, Enterprise found an outlet in choosing stories and themes that probably would not have been made at the big studios. One such was *Body and Soul*, which turned out to be the single biggest money maker for Enterprise, and Garfield was an important asset to the company. Interestingly, Enterprise was a studio without a traditional administrative hierarchy of studio chief and production heads. Aldrich felt, "Enterprise embodied a really brilliant idea of a communal way to make films. It was a brand-new departure, the first time I can remember that independent filmmakers had all the money they needed."

The concept did not produce the kind of masterpiece of film art that was hoped for, but Aldrich said, "For about two or three years before it went down the drain, I would guess that it had a better esprit de corps, and more interest and excitment going for it among its employees, from the laborer to the star, than any place in Hollywood. When, as they inevitably must, people began to realize the end product wasn't worth all this extra care and concern, the bubble burst and the dream faded."

Abraham Polonsky was another writer-director who worked at Enterprise. To him, Enterprise "was a great missed chance, but Hollywood is the capital of missed chances and strange victories. I imagine they go together in the indignity of history. In any event, the Blacklist would've crushed Enterprise." Polonsky characterized the social-film movement in the United States at that time as "a generalized political awareness existing in a number of people who were trying to make films that reflected this in one way or another when they had the opportunity to do so."

Garfield had involved himself in what he felt was a world of important filmmaking. Of his last seven films made as an independent, at least five could be said to deal with socially relevant themes, involving problems of contemporary society. Also, out of the seven, four rank among the best work of his career. Certainly, the most mature performances he gave were in *Body and Soul, Force of Evil, The Breaking Point,* and *He Ran All the Way*; the last was by far his most varied and forceful acting portrayal.

The films he wanted to make followed this general pattern. At one time he owned the rights to Nelson Algren's *The Man with the Golden Arm,* the story of a drug addict. The taboos against filming the book in 1950 were great, but Garfield wanted to do it. In *Conversations with Nelson Algren,* the author recalled, "I was edified that Garfield was so personal about it. His feeling was so personal about it. He liked the guy, Frankie Machine. He wanted to be Frankie Machine. He genuinely like this guy and the part. I was influenced by that. I mean I was very gratified that a good actor should want to be the guy that I created."

By this time, Garfield was fully committed to film acting, aware that it was a powerful tool. Through the film work of these final years he left a legacy of quality acting that is as exciting to watch today as it was then.

With Anne Revere

BODY AND SOUL
1947

Director, Robert Rossen; *producer,* Bob Roberts; *script,* Abraham Polonsky; *art director,* Nathan Juran; *music director,* Rudolph Polk; *cameraman,* James Wong Howe; *editor,* Francis Lyon; *released, August 22, 1947; running time,* 104 minutes; Enterprise Productions; released through United Artists.

CAST: John Garfield, Lilli Palmer, Hazel Brooks, Anne Revere, William Conrad, Art Smith, Lloyd Goff, Joseph Pevney, Canada Lee, James Burke, Virginia Gregg, Peter Virgo, Joe Devlin, Mary Currier, Milton Kibbee, Artie Dorrell, Cy Ring.

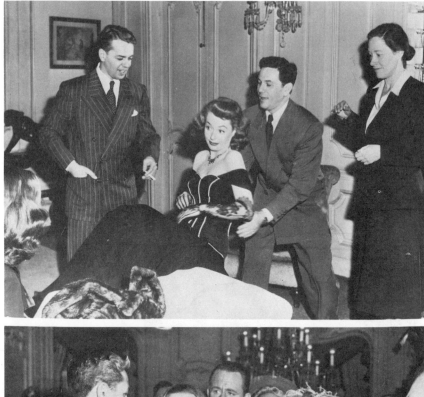

With Joseph Pevney, Lilli Palmer, and Anne Revere

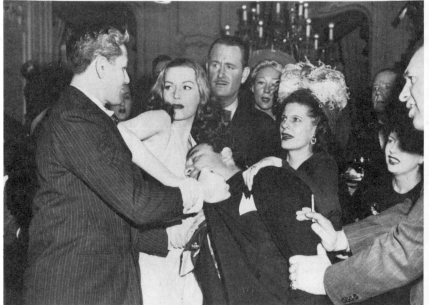

With Hazel Brooks

150

This film marked an important first for Garfield. As co-producer with Bob Roberts and working through Enterprise Productions, he was venturing into an area previously occupied by the studio or the well-known independent producer. There are other interesting aspects to the film: it was only the second directing assignment for Robert Rossen, who had been a well-known writer at Warners and had worked on several of Garfield's films there; it also marked a major screen credit for Polonsky (in those days the use of an original screenplay was rare).

Garfield was using his own money and knowledge to back his talent and the talent of the people assembled around him. He had not lost his touch, for *Body and Soul* was a financial and critical success. During the release of the film Garfield involved himself in a strenuous promotional tour. (The events of that period seem to have provided the material for the fictional biography based on his life. By focusing on these events, the novelist failed to see the major crisis point in Garfield's life.)

In some ways the film might be seen as a conservative choice for a first venture; the character, the milieu, the setting were all tried-and-true ground for him. It could be noted that he had made this film several times before. But although the story of a prizefighter who claws his way to the top bore resemblances to many earlier Garfield films, this time the focus was on corruption and the perversion of values that had once been thought of as honest and necessary. It is the story of Charlie Davis, the prizefighter who sacrifices his family, friends, and love for the material success that buys him glory and status. In some ways it was another variation of the *Golden Boy* theme but done, through the camera work of James Wong Howe, with a keener sense of realism.

With Anne Revere and Lilli Palmer

The film is not without flaws; there is in some scenes too great an emphasis on pictorial elements, and Lilli Palmer, though cast specifically because of her non-American exoticism, seems glaringly out of place in this setting.

Interestingly, the film was released in a period when at least three excellent films on prizefighting were made. The other two were *The Champion* and *The Setup*. The latter, starring Robert Ryan, was in some ways the best of the three.

Synopsis:

Charlie Davis (John Garfield), a young man of the slums, is determined to be a success. Teaming with Roberts, a gambler and fight promoter, Charlie uses his prowess as a boxer to achieve all his dreams of material wealth and fame. His quest for money and glory leads to the alienation of those closest to him. His best friend, Shorty, is killed, and he is estranged from his mother and the woman who loves him. His final act of corruption, deliberately losing a fight at Roberts's request, is a turning point. He decides to win, going against the gambler and the mob and starting out anew.

William Conrad oversees the boxer's examination

With James Wong Howe

153

With Peter Virgo, Joseph Pevney, Lloyd Gough, and Lilli Palmer

Garfield and Lloyd Gough standing over a prostrate Canada Lee

154

With Artie Darrell in the ring

Reviews:

The New York Times,
November 10, 1947:

After all the assorted prizefight pictures that have been paraded across the screen . . . it hardly seemed likely that another could possibly come along with enough zing and character to captivate and excite us for two hours. Yet "Body and Soul" has up and done it. . . . And John Garfield gives a rattling good performance as the steel-trap fighter through whose dissipated mind there flashes his career of money-chasing and bland two-timing on the eve of his last go. . . . Mr. Garfield really acts like the fresh kid who thinks the whole world is an easy set-up.

New York PM,
November 10, 1947:

"Body and Soul" has decided to say it again. By saying it with flourish, by milking it, by assembling for it a right-looking cast, by giving it an attention-arresting beginning and a magnificent fight climax—most of all by giving it one shattering touch of truth in the heart-breaking performance of Canada Lee, "Body and Soul" has managed to make the old statement seem vital and vigorous. . . . And, John Garfield, The Tension Kid, is wound up every minute, reacting exactly right.

With Gregory Peck, Celeste Holm, and Robert Karns

GENTLEMAN'S AGREEMENT

1947

Director, Elia Kazan; *producer*, Daryl F. Zanuck;
art directors, Lyle Wheeler, Mark-Lee Kirk; *script*, Moss
Hart from the book by Laura Z. Hobson; *music,*
Alfred Newman; *cameraman*, Arthur Miller; *editor*,
Harmon Jones; *released, November 1947*; *running
time*, 118 mins.; Twentieth-Century Fox.

CAST: Gregory Peck, John Garfield, Dorothy McGuire,
Celeste Holm, Ann Revere, June Havoc, Albert
Dekker, Jane Wyatt, Dean Stockwell, Nicholas Joy,
Sam Jaffe, Harold Vermilyea, Ransom M. Sherman,
Roy Roberts, Kathleen Lockhart, Curt Conway,
John Newland, Robert Warwick.

This was a small role for Garfield as the Jewish
soldier and friend of Gregory Peck, a writer who
is investigating anti-Semitism. Garfield's part was one-
dimensional and he took it because he considered
the subject "important." He said, "I didn't have to
act this one, I felt it."

In retrospect, the film seems curiously mild and
abstract in its treatment of such controversial material.
In view of the violence and hideousness of world
anti-Semitism in the twentieth century, such curiosities
as hotel ostracism, medical school quotas and country
club exclusiveness seem ineffectual and meaningless.
The film also deals with anti-Semitism from the point
of view of a Christian posing as a Jew; Gregory Peck
posing as a Jew comes in contact with the mildest
forms of prejudice, more irritating than destructive.
Coming after the events of World War II and Nazi
Germany, this glossy, sentimental and surface treatment
of anti-Semitism is particularly disturbing, for at the
time it was made it was considered a breakthrough
in Hollywood.

Synopsis:

Gregory Peck is a magazine writer who is working
on a series of articles exposing anti-Semitism. In
order to get firsthand and newsworthy material, he
decides to pose as a Jew. With the aid of his editor,
he is able to establish his new identity. In this new
life, the journalist is exposed to prejudice from all
sides: his fianceé, his friends, anonymous hotel clerks
and doctors, and even Jewish co-workers. His mother
and son are also exposed to prejudice. At the close,
he decides that it is only fair-minded and intelligent
people who can combat anti-Semitism.

Reviews:

The New York Times,
November 12, 1947:

John Garfield's performance of a young Jew,
lifelong friend of the hero, is a bit too mechanical.

Time,
November 17, 1947:

Kazan's sure hand has bottled John Garfield's
carbonated talent into a clear, constrained performance
as the hero's Jewish friend.

With Roy Roberts

158

FORCE OF EVIL
1948

Director, Abraham Polonsky; *producer,* Bob Roberts; *script, Abraham Polonsky and Ira Wolfert, from the* book *Tuckers People,* by Ira Wolfert; *art director,* Richard Day; *music director,* Rudolph Polk; *cameraman,* George Barnes; *editor,* Art Seid; *released, December 1948; running time,* 78 minutes; Enterprise Productions; released through MGM.

CAST: John Garfield, Beatrice Pearson, Thomas Gomez, Roy Roberts, Marie Windsor, Howard Chamberlain, Paul McVey, Jack Overman, Tim Ryan, Barbara Woodell, Raymond Largay, Stanley Prager, Beau Bridges, Allan Mathews, Barry Kelley, Paul Fix, Georgia Backus, Sid Tomak, Sid Stone.

With Roy Roberts

With Beatrice Pearson

With Miss Pearson

160

A passed over film, *Force of Evil* was revived with some audience success on television in the fifties and, mainly through the career of its blacklisted director, has had a loyal following in critical circles. In some ways the film is a measure of Garfield's desire to tackle material that avoids the cliché endings that marred much of his earlier work at Warners, while dealing with a smiliar screen characterization. Though the criticism could be made that his film roles were essentially stereotyped, it is important to see that he attempted to develop that character in deeper and more meaningful situations, and thus lift it out of confining clichés.

In fact, *Force of Evil* turns all the clichés upside-down—the ghetto achiever uses socially acceptable values to distort and corrupt himself and those around him, and seemingly innocent people doing honest work are seen as manipulated by corrupt forces in their environment. In total, the film attempts a realistic view of the ghetto without the nostalgia and romanticism that earlier films used to distort the picture.

It focuses on the corruption of a young syndicate lawyer, Joe Marsh, who measures success purely in terms of money. But he lives in a world in which everyone is tainted by crime and corruption, even the average people—bookkeepers, secretaries, and workers. Joe Marsh symbolizes this pervasive evil pushed to its farthest limit. With each step deeper into corruption, he destroys someone close to him, someone he loves. He must reject it in order to live again.

Synopsis:

Two brothers find themselves on opposite sides in the policy-numbers racket. The younger brother, Joe Morse (John Garfield), is a lawyer for the syndicate and has masterminded an elaborate takeover of all the small operators in the city for Tucker, the syndicate chief. His older brother, Leo, is one of those small operators and is against the takeover, even though he has been offered a lucrative job.

Leo measures his brother's act in terms of small evils against larger ones. Joe, unable to convince his brother, goes ahead with the plan, confident that once there is no other alternative, Leo will come to him. When Leo resists, Tucker has him killed, and in revenge Joe decides to divulge all to the new reform district attorney.

Review:

The New York Times,
December 27, 1948:

Out of material and ideas that have been worked over time after time, so that they've long since become stale and hackneyed, [*Force of Evil*] gathers suspense and dread, a genuine feeling of the bleakness of crime and a terrible sense of doom. True, [Polonsky] was very fortunate in having John Garfield play the young lawyer in the story, for Mr. Garfield is his tough guy self to the life. Sentient underneath a steel shell, taut, articulate—he is all good men gone wrong.

With Gilbert Roland and Jennifer Jones

WE WERE STRANGERS
1949

Director, John Huston; *producer*, S. P. Eagle; *script*, Peter Viertel and John Huston, from an episode in the book *Rough Sketch*, by Robert Sylvester; *cameraman*, Russell Metty; *editor*, Al Clark; *released*, May 1949; *running time*, 106 minutes; Horizon Productions; released through Columbia Pictures.

CAST: John Garfield, Jennifer Jones, Gilbert Roland, Pedro Armendariz.

This was Garfield's first film for John Huston, who had recently finished his critically acclaimed *Treasure of*

the Sierra Madre. The theme had immediate political overtones; it was set in revolutionary Cuba of 1933, with Garfield as an American-born Cuban returned to lead a guerrilla undertaking. The premise, that the revolutionaries must kill many innocent people in order to start the revolution, was provocative. However, the story, the dialogue, the direction, and Garfield's acting never came together.

All the elements of a typical Huston plot were present: A group of men band together to perform a dangerous task; they work together at first, there is dissension, and as they are on the verge of success, the entire affair is dissipated by outside forces. The strong political questions raised in the early part of the film were also dissipated by the final scenes. Garfield's

character seemed stiff and uneasy, and he had difficulty handling the pseudo-Hemingway dialogue. Such lines as "The tomb is not the end; it is merely the way" were clumsy and ineffectual for him.

The film was attacked by both right- and left-wing press, called communist-inspired by the former and denounced as capitalist-propaganda by the latter. It is interesting that Huston was a leader in the formation of the Committee for the First Amendment, and Garfield was one of its early supporters.

Both Garfield and Huston wanted to test an unknown actress, Marilyn Monroe, for the leading female role. They set up the test but were stopped by producer Sam Spiegel. Huston used Monroe in his next film, *The Asphalt Jungle*.

Synopsis:

Tony Fenner (John Garfield) is a Cuban-born American who has returned to the island in 1933 to help instigate an armed revolution. With help from an underground organization, he has concocted an elaborate plan to lure high government officials to a funeral and blow them up by planting explosives in a tunnel underneath the cemetery.*

The four men work on the tunnel until one of them cracks under the mental strain and almost destroys the plan. He had been distressed because many innocent people would be killed in the explosion. Fenner sees only the revolutionary end that his plan will achieve and works the men toward that goal. At the instant the plan is to be put into effect, however, the government changes the funeral arrangements and the police close in on Fenner and his comrades.

Fenner is killed fighting the police, but at the moment when he seems to have lost, the sounds of gunfire initiating the revolution can be heard.

* Interestingly, a similar plan was actually used to blow up the car of the leading heir to General Franco in Spain.

Review:

The New York Times,
April 28, 1949:

A fancied attempt at insurrection against the dictatorial regime of President Machado in Cuba back in 1933 is wrought by director Huston into a dark, desperate melodramatic tale. . . . But somehow, the real emotional tinder which is scattered within this episode is never swept into a pyramid and touched off with a quick, explosive spark. . . . The cold, calculating perseverance of the young American leader of the group is clinched in the eternal tension of John Garfield in the principal role.

With Orley Lindgren and Micheline Presle

UNDER MY SKIN
1950

Director, Jean Negulesco; *producer*, Casey Robinson; *script*, Casey Robinson, from Ernest Hemingway's story "My Old Man"; *music*, Daniele Amfetheatrol; *art directors*, Lyle Wheeler and Maurice Ransford; *cameraman*, Joseph La Shelle; *editor*, Dorothy Spencer; *released, March 1950; running time,* 86 minutes; 20th Century-Fox.

CAST: John Garfield, Micheline Presle, Luther Adler, Orley Lindgren, Noel Drayton, A. A. Merola, Ott George, Paul Bryar, Ann Codee, Steve Geray, Joseph Warfield, Eugene Borden, Loulette Sablon, Alphonse Martell.

With Noel Drayton

With Paul Bryar and Luther Adler

This was Garfield's third film with director Negulesco, which, aside from his work with Curtiz, stands as a sustained working relationship in Hollywood. Yet Negulesco's direction is at odds with Garfield's realistic style of acting, and the Negulesco-directed stories always seemed too tame for the actor. In this case, location shooting in Europe, an Ernest Hemingway story, and Group Theatre ally Luther Adler could not redeem the confusion of approach. The story of a jockey and his son who roam the race tracks of Europe, with a keener eye for women than for horses, needed action direction to get the authentic Hemingway touch.

Their three films together seemed a strange departure for both men, whose film careers had such different focal points. Negulesco, in an interview, passed over this film rather quickly and noted of Garfield, "He led a rough life and burned himself out."

Synopsis:

As a crooked jockey, barred from racing in Italy and the United States, John Garfield goes to France to try his luck. His young son does not know the truth about his father and idolizes him. The jockey is involved with many women, including a nightclub singer (Micheline Presle). He rides honest races until a former associate shows up and pressures him into one more crooked deal.

The son soon learns that his father is dishonest and cruel. This shocks the father, who tries to redeem himself in his son's eyes. On the verge of making up for his past, he is accidentally injured while racing and dies.

Review:

The New York Times,
March 18, 1950:

The germ of a devastating drama which Ernest Hemingway conveyed in his story of a crooked jockey and his little boy under the title "My Old Man" has been pretty well doused with antiseptics. . . . The jockey, played by John Garfield, is a bumptious and brutish sort of a chap who spends more time acting wolfish . . . than he spends in pursuit of his career.

THE DIFFICULT YEARS
1950

Director, Luigi Zampa; *screenplay* by Sergio Amidei, Vitalinao Brancati, Franco Evangelistii, and Enrico Fulchegnono, based on the novel by Vitalinao Brancati; *English version* by Arthur Miller, *narrated* by John Garfield. Released by Lopert Films Inc.

An unusual combination of narration written by Arthur Miller and spoken by John Garfield contributed to one of the first antifascist films to come out of Italy. Miller and Garfield were outspoken antifascists and probably contributed their services on that basis. Unfortunately, the English version seems unavailable today, and the *New York Times* review noted: "The urge to support the national [Italian] ego is most evident in 'The Difficult Years' an odd little job of introspection . . . [that] tells the story of a little Sicilian government clerk who is trapped and destroyed by fascism after the critical year 1934. . . . An English commentary by Arthur Miller which John Garfield now and then speaks contributed no more to understanding than the English subtitles for the dialogue."

THE BREAKING POINT
1950

Director, Michael Curtiz; *producer,* Jerry Wald; *script,*
Ranald MacDougall, from the Ernest Hemingway book
To Have and Have Not; *cameraman,* Ted McCord;
editor, Alan Crosslands; *released, September 30, 1950;*
running time, 97 minutes; Warner Bros.

CAST: John Garfield, Patricia Neal, Phyllis Thaxter,
Juano Hernandez, Wallace Ford, Edmond Ryan,
Ralphe Dumke.

With Wallace Ford

With Phyllis Thaxter

Garfield was teamed again with a director who always brought out the best in his acting style—Michael Curtiz. An earlier filming of Hemingway's story *To Have and Have Not* had been done as a vehicle for Humphrey Bogart and Lauren Bacall. Aside from resetting it on the California coast, MacDougall's version was much closer to the Hemingway original. It was a very simple story, highly realistic and with no pretensions—the kind Garfield worked best at. Garfield responded well to the character of Harry Morgan, the strong man undermined by his own weaknesses.

As with most Curtiz films, the casting was excellent: Phyllis Thaxter as Morgan's wife, a dowdy-looking woman whose secret is the sexual attraction she feels toward her man; Patricia Neal as the free-wheeling, husky-voiced prostitute; Wallace Ford, a fat, seedy Mexican divorce lawyer; Juano Hernandez, Morgan's black friend and co-worker.

In this film Garfield has dropped his old mannerisms of shouting and finger jabbing, and his performance is totally under control. The scene where his wife catches him secretly pocketing a gun is a good example of

Garfield's ability to gain dimension as an actor. He makes a show at trying to convince her that he knows what he is doing; then he bullies her, his voice curt and sharp—but through it all he avoids her gaze, his expression is guilt ridden, and his hands are limp.

The end sequence, too, is a brilliant tour de force in action direction. It is a complex arrangement of angles, set-ups, and cutting, as Garfield shoots it out with the robbers aboard a moving fishing boat. Garfield's acting brings it off in believable style, as more foolish than heroic.

Curtiz's final touch, however, lifts the film above any individual acting performance. Morgan's friend has been killed, and he is near death as the boat returns to the dock with the coast guard. Morgan's wife and family rush to him; we see him in his final moments. The crowd at the dock leaves as the ambulance takes Morgan off. The scene is empty except for a lone black child—the son of Morgan's dead friend. The little boy stands motionless on the dock looking at the boat, waiting for his father, as the camera pulls away.

With Patricia Neal

With Juano Hernandez   173

With Patricia Neal and Juano Hernandez

With Phyllis Thaxter

Synopsis:

Harry Morgan (John Garfield) is a hard-pressed owner of a sport-fishing boat on the California coast. He barely earns his payments and food for his family by taking wealthy businessmen on fishing trips. With his friend and co-worker (Juano Hernandez), he takes a so-called businessman and his girlfriend (Patricia Neal) on a fishing trip with a stopover in Mexico. There, the businessman runs out, leaving Morgan with a lot of bills and the girlfriend. Morgan decides to take a boatload of Chinese illegally into the United States. When he is cheated out of his money, Morgan is forced to kill the leader and dump the others on the beach.

Back home in California, the coast guard has been informed of Morgan's adventures and confiscates his boat. Desperate for money, Morgan takes another deal with the crooked lawyer (Wallace Ford) who set up the first one. This time he must take a group of shady characters to an island outside the international limits. The men have robbed a racetrack and plan to kill Morgan when they no longer need him. In a shootout, after Morgan has got his friend killed, he manages to dispose of all the thieves and is fatally wounded himself.

Reviews:

The New York Times,
October 7, 1950:

Warner Brothers, which has already taken one feeble swing and a cut at Ernest Hemingway's memorable story of a tough guy, "To Have and Have Not," finally has got hold of that fable and socked it for a four-base hit in a film called "The Breaking Point." . . . All the character, color, and cynicism of Mr. Hemingway's lean and hungry tale are wrapped up in this realistic picture, and John Garfield is tops in the principal role. . . . Mr. Garfield is a big help in this respect—all through his playing of Harry Morgan is the shrewdest, hardest acting in the show.

New York Daily News,
October 7, 1950:

Hemingway or no Hemingway, "To Have and Have Not" turned out to be a good adventure film, with Humphrey Bogart and Lauren Bacall in the leading roles. "The Breaking Point" comes closer to the original and is a more serious drama. . . .

As good as Garfield is in the part, he could use a role at this stage of his screen career in which he didn't have to display a disagreeable disposition. It seems that he has become a victim of the Hollywood habit of type casting.

With Shelley Winters, Bobby Hyatt and Wallace Ford

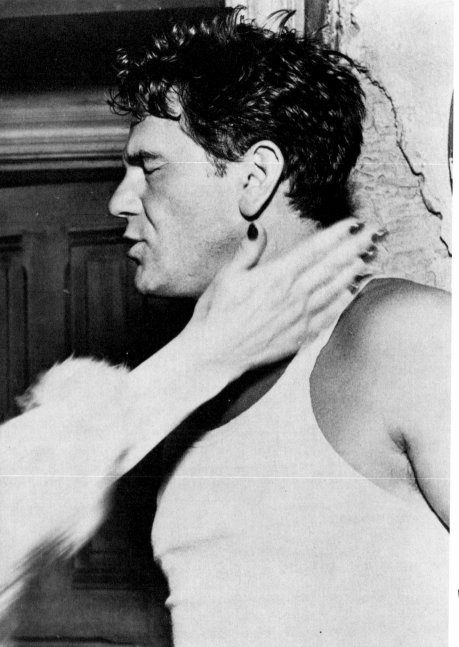

With Gladys George

HE RAN ALL THE WAY
1951

Director, John Berry; *producer*, Bob Roberts; *associate producer*, Paul Trivers; *script*, Hugo Butler and Guy Endore, from the book by Sam Bass; *music*, Franz Waxman; *cameraman*, James Wong Howe; *editor*, Francis D. Lyon; *released, July 13, 1951; running time*, 77 minutes; Enterprise Studios; released through United Artists.

CAST: John Garfield, Wallace Ford, Shelley Winters, Selene Royle, Gladys George, Norman Lloyd, Bobby Hyatt.

With Wallace Ford, Bobby Hyatt, Shelley Winters, and Selena Royle

With Shelley Wint

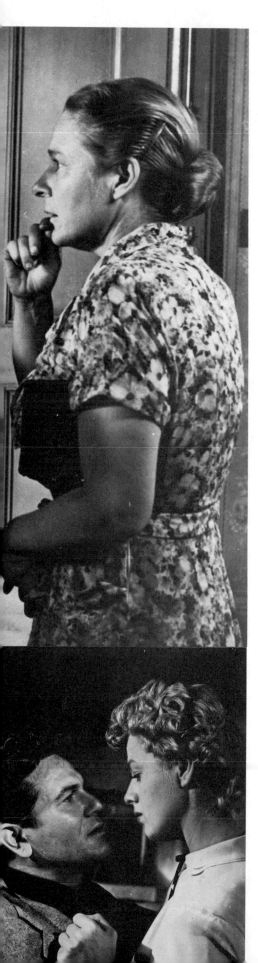

This was the last and best of Garfield's screen performances. His work is matched by first-rate acting from the whole cast, fast-paced direction, restrained and powerful camera work, and a tense musical score that enhances the emotional impact of individual scenes. Garfield plays a slightly dumb strong man, a tough guy who lacks the confidence of his physical strength. In an opening sequence, his friend tells him before planning a holdup, "You think slow, Nick—you move fast, but you think slow." There is ample scope for Garfield's brooding physical intensity in this portrayal of a trapped thief, more wounded animal than cold-blooded killer.

The setting is also interesting, for this was one of the first films to use the theme of a family trapped in its own home by hostile outside forces—a device that would become familiar in fifties films. In some ways the movie is like the later film *The Desperate Hours*, but this version varies one of the key elements. Instead of involving a middle-class family and the familiar suburban background, this story takes place in the apartment of a working-class family. Because the killer and the family share the same background, the ambivalence of their relationship is both believable and dramatic. In this film, Garfield, as the killer who is rejected by his own family, tries to become a part of the family he terrorizes.

This ambivalence between the killer and his prey is a necessary plot device that also adds complexity to the characters. It makes the love relationship between the daughter (played sympathetically by Shelley Winters) and the killer believable. And in the final explosive sequence in which she shoots him, the visual setting of tenement flats, winding staircases, and rain-splashed streets gives one of the most effective endings of all Garfield's films.

Some of the other interesting elements in the film include a tense holdup sequence with excellent integration of camera and musical effects, a subtle performance by Wallace Ford as the father (Ford was an excellent and little-noticed character actor of the period), and an emotionally powerful performance by child actor Bobby Hyatt. Unfortunately, the film has been generally unnoticed, except for occasional television screening, but it is both an important genre film and a thoroughly entertaining story.

Synopsis:

Nick Rocco (John Garfield) is a small-time thief, not very smart and not very brave. At the instigation of his friend Al, Nick joins him in a payroll robbery. The thieves panic, and in the confusion a guard and Al are

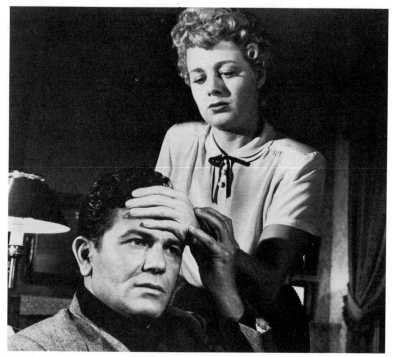

With Shelley Winters

wounded. Nick escapes with the money and hides at a nearby public swimming pool.

When the pool closes, Nick latches on to a girl he had met there (Shelley Winters). He takes her home, where he meets her father, mother, and younger brother. The family goes to a movie, and Nick and the girl remain in the apartment. When the family returns, he thinks they have found out about him, and he holds them at gunpoint in a moment of panic.

Later he tells them that he will leave in the morning, but when the morning paper arrives he finds that the guard is dead and he is wanted for murder. He holds the family hostage, alternately befriending and terrorizing them, unsure of himself and unable to move from the small apartment.

He is able to trust only the girl and decides to give her money for a car so they can both escape. The father leaves the house vowing to stop them. When the car does not arrive, Nick panics again, this time turning on the girl. He forces her out of the apartment, where her father stands, ready to kill Nick. For a moment the girl must choose between her father and her lover; she shoots Nick. At that moment the car arrives that would have taken them both away.

Reviews:

The New York Times,
June 21, 1951:

Beyond any question, Hugo Butler and Guy Endore

have penned a shock-crammed script from Sam Ross' mordent novel upon which the picture is based. From the first splattering scene in which the hero is roundly slapped by his own hateful ma, through the misfired stickup and subsequent hideout, brutality is piled upon surprise. John Berry's driving direction is designed to further punctuation of shock, with Franz Waxman's music and sound tricks adding an apt cacophony. Further, John Garfield's stark performance as the fugitive who desperately contrives to save himself briefly from capture is full of startling glints from start to end. He makes a most odd and troubled creature unused to the normal flow of life. . . . And in Mr. Garfield's performance, vis-a-vis the rest of the cast, is conveyed a small measure of the irony and pity that was in the book.

Variety,
June 6, 1951:

"He Ran All the Way" is a taut gangster pic. Good production values keep a routine yarn fresh and appealing. Film is scripted, played and directed all the way with little waste motion, so that the suspense is steady and interest constantly sustained.

Garfield is highly effective as a harshly-raised hoodlum filled with some decent emotions, confused by the affection the invaded family has for each other. . . .

(Overleaf) The end of Nick Rocco

Chapter 3: The Theater
STAGE CAREER

The dominant influence on Garfield's early professional life was his association with the people who made up the Group Theatre. They were a close-knit gathering, mainly New Yorkers with one or two outsiders admitted to the inner circle. Intense and dedicated, they were an irritant on the New York theater scene because they wouldn't play the game by the old rules, insisting on doing financially unrewarding plays with a repertory approach, rotating assignments, even turning down lucrative parts to perform together, and what's more, seriously believing in what they were doing. Not everyone looked on them favorably. They were once described as "that strange, but not untalented agglomeration of idealists, communists, sex perverts, and opportunists." To others, such as the playwright Paul Green, they were "in many ways wonderful. And of course the fervor of the Group Theatre acting, the lyrical power in it, was usually much above the average. And Lord, how they worked at it!" By 1935 they were in the forefront of the intellectual and avant-garde movement in New York.

The years before joining the Group were Garfield's apprenticeship—studies with Maria Ouspenskaya and Richard Boleslavsky, bit parts in shows, and work in Eve Le Gallienne's Civic Repertory. In the summer of 1934, when he went to Ellenville as an apprentice with the Group, his indoctrination began in the focal point of their work—the Method. The Method was one of their chief distinctions; it was a system of acting technique derived from the theories of Stanislavsky and practiced fervently by such theater lights as Lee Strasberg, Stella Adler, Harold Clurman, and Morris Carnovsky. Their work with it was an important influence on American theater, for the Method soon became the dominant form of actor training in this country. It wasn't a system that could be put down on paper, for it depended a good deal on the interaction between the actors and the director.

That summer of '34 the Group was deeply committed to the Method, as if to some cabalistic rite. Paul Green, who was both sympathetic to and irritated by their system, described the Method approach: "The directors would take a particular actor or actress and say, 'Here's a part in a play or here's a page, a little piece of a scene. Now you go off over there by that tree and lean your head up against the tree and do all you can to bring a feeling, an experience in your life that is similar to what the scene is about—an emotion—an emotional experience.' Emotion was a great word with them. They hardly ever used the word 'thought' or 'reason'—just emotion. . . . Of course, it was understood that if the emotion was intense enough, all the rest flowed in and

Elia Kazan as an actor about 1935

Luther Adler appearing in Beggars Are Coming to Town

Stella Adler in John Howard Lawson's Gentlewoman

J. Edward Bromberg about 1936

Lee J. Cobb during 1952 run of Golden Boy

Clifford Odets, about 1938

forward, I guess. . . . Now that I look back on it, it was good, maybe even some greatness in it."

To an actor who relied solely on technique—the precise manipulation of body and voice—the Method was anathema. The opposing points of view provided a schism in the approach to acting—was it primarily a physical task to be learned through exercise, control, and practice, or was it first an emotional attunement of the actor in which he could duplicate the experience of the role? In *The Fervent Years*, a reminiscence and evaluation of the Group, Harold Clurman described the Method as being two related approaches. The first was "improvisation," in which the actor performs extemporaneously scenes that are emotionally analogous to those in the play; the second is called "affective memory," or the use of one's emotional experience from the past to fill in the details of a similar emotional experience within the play. It has always seemed inherent in the Method that through the system, an actor could transform himself into the role in a way that mere technique could not approximate. It was this belief that produced the fervor and dedication of its main practitioners. From 1934 to 1938 Garfield ate, slept, and dreamed the Method, and, more importantly, he worked as a Method actor.

Another distinction of the Group Theatre was its reliance on ensemble performance; it admitted members only after a thorough examination of their working abilities. To outsiders this attitude was cliquish and exclusive, and in some instances it was, but it also was in direct opposition to the dominant Broadway approach that treated each play as a new start. The Group was a repertory company, but instead of performing the classics, they were committed to new playwrights and new forms in the theater. They saw themselves as innovators, rather than traditionalists. This attitude colored all Garfield's work in the theater. The plays he worked on when he returned to New York in the late forties were always termed "experimental," "controversial," or "important," and his approach was to work for little money in a role that he felt was significant and demanding.

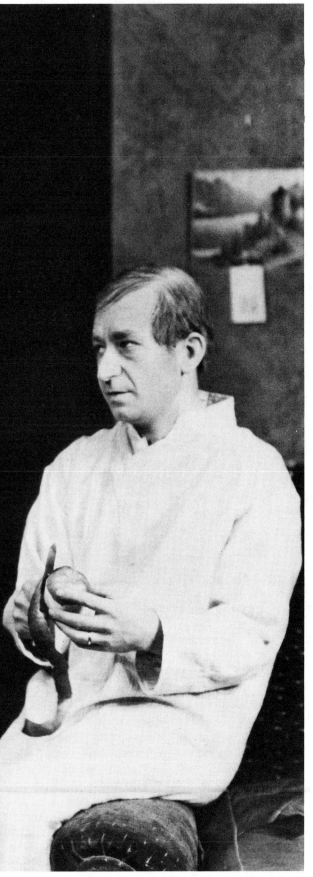

With Luther Adler, Phoebe Brand and Art Smith

AWAKE AND SING
1935

Author, Clifford Odets; *director,* Harold Clurman; *setting,* Boris Aronson; *produced* by the Group Theatre, at the Belasco Theatre; opened, February 19, 1935.

CAST: Art Smith, Stella Adler, Morris Carnovsky, Phoebe Brand, Jules Garfield, Roman Bohnen, Luther Adler, J. Edward Bromberg, Sanford Meisner.

This is the story of the Berger family, working-class immigrants with their American-born children, just barely living in the ghettos of the Bronx. It takes place in their suffocatingly small apartment; the mother and father trying desperately to find a suitable husband for the pregnant daughter and to prevent their son from moving and breathing, from making his own mistakes. In their world, one mistake means the end.

As Ralph Berger, the young son, Garfield would fit the author's description: "Ralph is a boy with a clean spirit. He wants to know, wants to learn. He is ardent, he is romantic, he is sensitive. He is naïve too. He is trying to find why so much dirt must be cleared away before it is possible to 'get to first base.' "

With Luther Adler and Morris Carnovsky

The only small liberating force is the grandfather, who once had ideals and a desire for action and change but is now kept in tow in his daughter's house. He commits suicide in order to allow Ralph to live, but it is his books, not the insurance money, that are Ralph's legacy.

The New York Times critic noted, "After experimenting with scripts of several different kinds, the Group Theatre has found its most congenial playwright under its own roof, Clifford Odets. . . . He has written in three acts a vigorous and closely matted drama of Jewish life in the Bronx, and nine members of the Group Theatre play it with stunning power. . . . Jules

Garfield plays the part of the boy with a splendid sense of character development."

This was Garfield's first important role in the theater. He had been on trial with the Group up to this time, and this was the chance to prove himself. Just before the last performance of the show, Harold Clurman came into his dressing room and told him he had been accepted as a full member. A friend recalled that he broke down completely and they had to hold the curtain for ten minutes until he recovered. Years later in Hollywood, Garfield would say that nothing as good as that had happened to him before or since.

WEEP FOR THE VIRGINS
1935

Author, Nellise Child; *director*, Cheryl Crawford; *settings*, Boris Aronson; *produced by the* Group Theatre, at the 46th Street Theatre; opened, December 1, 1935.

CAST: Eunice Stoddard, Art Smith, J. Edward Bromberg, Tony Kraber, Margaret Barker, Ruth Nelson, Phoebe Brand, Paula Miller, Evelyn Varden, Hilda Reis, Alexander Kirkland, Mildred Van Dorn, William Nicholas, Jules Garfield, Virginia Stevens, Marie Hunt, Dorothy Patten.

The setting of this play took the Group actors far afield, to San Diego, with a background of the canneries and down-and-out life on the West Coast—a milieu Steinbeck would popularize in the thirties. The plot revolved again around a family whose every member dreamed of escaping the squalid surroundings, each one building a fairy tale of fantastic hope and impossible goals. One will make his fortune with a frog farm; another entertains an equally impossible dream of Hollywood success. Garfield's part as a young sailor who enters the life of one of the daughters was short but noteworthy.

The play was rehearsed at the same time as Odets's *Paradise Lost*, which was of more immediate interest to the Group. All the participants seemed to have misgivings about the production. One reviewer noted, "Although the production includes an imaginative setting by Boris Aronson and several excellent bits of individual acting, it is difficult to understand what drew the Group Theatre into staging this script." The play was more a failure for the Group than for the actors involved.

HAVING WONDERFUL TIME
1937

Author, Arthur Kober; *director* and *producer*, Marc Connelly; *setting*, Stewart Chaney; opened at the Lyceum Theatre, February 21, 1937.

CAST: B. D. Kranz, Mona Conrad, Ann Thomas, Irving Israel, Henrietta Kaye, Connie Lent, Tony Kraber, Ann Brody, Mitchell Grayson, Kay Loring, Phillip Van Zandt, Jules Garfield, Sidney Fox, Hudy Block, Katherine Locke, Louise Reichard, Herbert Ratner, William Sweetland, Sheldon Leonard, Lilly Windton, Rank Gould.

This was Garfield's first acting role outside the Group in more than three years. It was an establishment Broadway hit, a high-spirited comedy on the antics of city dwellers on their summer vacations at the Catskill Mountain resorts. The protagonists were termed "hillbillies from the Bronx," and Garfield played a young law student working his way through college as a counselor at Camp Kare-free. It was a familiar role for him; although he had never been to college, he had frequented many Catskill resorts.

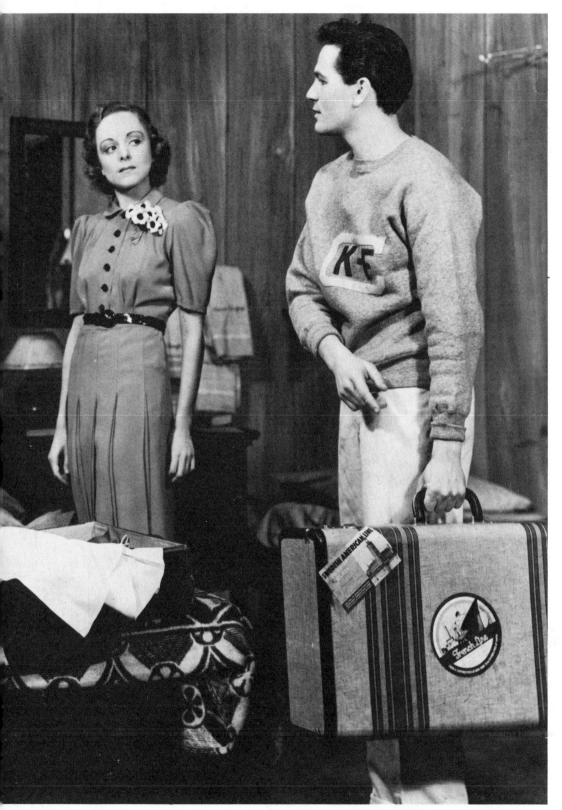

With Ann Thomas and Katherine Locke

With Katherine Locke

With Sidney Fox

As Chick Kessler, he delivered the right balance of comic naïveté and romantic boyishness. In one sense this was the idealized romantic view of the Ralph Berger character he had portrayed in the Odets play. In fact, that performance had brought him to the attention of director Marc Connelly. In this play the purpose was amusement, and Garfield could turn just the right emotional dials to shift the character to the humorous side of center. *The New York Times* reviewer marked it as a hit: "Perfectly cast and sensitively acted under Marc Connelly's direction, 'Having Wonderful Time' is not only amusing but tender, and a credit to the prevailing mood of good-will in the theatre."

With the success of the play, he had become something of an established actor on Broadway. "Jules Garfield has the sort of perceptions that make an admirable character of Chick Kessler, and he also knows how to convey them in the theatre," noted the *Times*.

He did not stay for the complete run of the play because "important" work with the Group always took precedence, and when the call came, he left.

With Phoebe Brand

GOLDEN BOY
1937

Author, Clifford Odets; director, Harold Clurman; *settings*, Mordecai Gorelik; *produced by the* Group Theatre, at the Belasco Theatre; opened, November 4, 1937.

CAST: Frances Farmer, Luther Adler, Roman Bohnen, Art Smith, Morris Carnovsky, Phoebe Brand, John O'Malley, Robert Lewis, Elia Kazan, Harry Bratsburg, Michael Gordon, Lee J. Cobb, Jules Garfield, Bert Conway, Martin Ritt, Charles Crisp, Howard da Silva, Charles Niemeyer, Karl Malden.

Having missed out on the title role, Garfield played the comic part of Siggie, the cabdriver. By now, he had proved his comic effectiveness on stage and was remembered by fellow Group members as "a comic actor with unusual flair."

The story centers on Joe Bonaparte, a young man of the streets who must choose between the life of a prize fighter, with its quest for instant fame and money, and the life of an artist, a musician, with no hope for money or glory, but only for the intrinsic values of his art.

The characters line up on one side or the other. Joe's father, who has lived only to see his son become a violinist, is pitted against Eddie Fuseli, the gangster (played chillingly by Elia Kazan) who owns Joe in the boxing ring. In the end, the Golden Boy chooses money and fame, and when he is killed in a car crash, only his father weeps for the potential that was lost.

The reviews singled the play out for success. "Although Clifford Odets's 'Golden Boy' has been a long time in the making, it is worth waiting for. As produced by the Group Theatre at the Belasco last evening it is a hardfisted piece of work about a prize fighter whose personal ambition turns into hatred of the world," noted *The New York Times*.

Garfield's role as the brother-in-law was more comic relief than central to the story. However, it is impossible to read the play without visualizing him as Joe Bonaparte. In a sense his identification with the role by those who remember the play is a refutation of Harold Clurman's feeling that although Garfield "was obviously the type, he had neither the pathos nor the variety, in my opinion, to sustain the role." It was a bitter disappointment for him, and he left in the middle of the run.

With Morris Carnovsky, who played the father

With Aline MacMahon and Harry Carey

HEAVENLY EXPRESS
1940

Author, Albert Bein; *director*, Robert Lewis; *setting and costumes*, Boris Aronson; *musical composer and arranger*, Lehman Engel; *produced by* Kermit Bloomgarden, at the National Theatre; opened, April 18, 1940.

CAST: John Garfield, Phil Brown, William Sands, Aline MacMahon, Harry Carey, Curt Conway, Harry Bratsburg, Randolph Wade, Will Lee, Philip Loeb, Russell Collins, James O'Rear, Nicholas Conte, Burl Ives, Jack Lambert, Charles Thompson.

This was Garfield's return to Broadway, now as a well-known actor in a leading role. *Heavenly Express* was completely different from the films and plays he had done before. It was musical fantasy and placed him, for the first time, outside the realistic style of acting. Essentially, Garfield was both limited and broadened by his work with the Group and in Hollywood. He did not have training in a wide variety of roles that a repertory actor would get. In American theater, then and now, there were not many opportunities for repertory work. Instead, Garfield learned his trade with the Group appearing in contemporary plays of social importance, where the Method proved an excellent tool for a realistic actor.

Heavenly Express was admittedly experimental. John Houseman, who had been involved in Bein's first play, *Li'l Ol' Boy,* liked *Express* but thought it unfinished. He noted, "It still was not right when it was produced on Broadway four years later. . . ." But Garfield, eager to use his contract clause and return to New York, and genuinely interested in the play, went ahead with the production. He had been given encouragement from Odets, who put his money into the production. With that enthusiasm, Garfield tackled the part of the Overland Kid, the mythical hobo death spirit who rides the rails seeking lonely hoboes to transport to heaven, with his usual energy. On stage, he strummed a mandolin and sang.

The *Times* reviewer liked the performance when other reviewers found it unsatisfactory. "Mr. Garfield plays with a glow of youth and a touch of Ariel—altogether the most winning angel of death in the theatre." He was attracted by the element in the play that made Garfield enthusiastic. "Call it 'experiment' because every part of the play is not equally vital or eloquent. But share in the joy of a number of theatre people who have expressed in the drama a freedom and exultation that pedestrian imitations of humanity cannot equal. It is creative."

John Mason Brown thought Garfield wrong for the part, even though he felt the play was new and experimental. To him, Garfield was "too well fed. . . . The last thing he suggests is a ticket taker on the eerie. He is likable enough, in an earth-bound way, when relaxed, and reads with genuine skill."

Garfield's return to Broadway as a leading performer had not been as triumphant as he had hoped. It would be eight years before he would perform on the New York stage again. In between he did work in various stage productions with the Laboratory Theatre in Los Angeles, and of course, the war years made it difficult to get back.

SKIPPER NEXT TO GOD
1948

Author, Jan De Hartog; *director*, Lee Strasberg; *setting*, Boris Aronson; *producer*, Cheryl Crawford; *presented by the* Experimental Theatre, under the sponsorhip of the American National Theatre and Academy, at the Maxine Elliott Theatre; opened, January 4, 1948.

CAST: John Garfield, Joseph Anthony, Robert White, Si Oakland, Carmen Costi, John Becker, Wallace Acton, Wolfe Barzell, Michael Lewin, Peter Kaas, John Shellie, Jabez Gray, Richard Coogan, Eugene Stuckman, Harry Irvine.

With John Shellie

As a drama of social and moral complexities, *Skipper Next to God* was the kind of play Garfield admired. It marked his return to New York theater. He had made several previous attempts to return, to do plays including a much-talked-about life of Nijinsky that Odets had wanted to write for him and, more recently, the part of Stanley in *Streetcar*. When Garfield rejected the latter play, he welcomed the chance to do *Skipper*. It was an experimental production in many ways, using student performers. He was reunited with former Group Theatre director Lee Strasberg and with Cheryl Crawford.

The plot involves the captain of a shipload of Jews bound for a South American port. When they are refused entry, the captain, a devout Christian, must fight his own crew and the authorities to achieve what he sees as his higher duty, safeguarding his passengers and securing their future. He finally decides to wreck the ship off the U.S. coast, to force the authorities to accept the Jews on land.

The subject was highly topical, coming after the massacre of Jews in Europe during the thirties and forties. However, the play relied heavily on argument and debate, which tended to dilute the drama. The critics bowed to the intensity of the subject, but they found the drama too intellectually engulfed in its own point of view. The *Times* critic said, "Whatever its merit may be Jan De Hartog's 'Skipper Next to God' deserves to be produced."

What little emotional impact there was in the play seems to have come through in Garfield's performance. The reviewer singled this point out: "Mr. Garfield filled the whole performance with vitality by the force, directness and perception of his acting as the captain. Apart from the depth of his understanding, Mr. Garfield is a fiery actor. He can also translate emotion into something egregious by portraying it too deliberately. . . . This is a fault in the right direction. For Mr. Garfield is an uncommonly enlightened actor who also can appreciate the ethics of a part."

With Nancy Kelly

THE BIG KNIFE
1949

Author, Clifford Odets; *director*, Lee Strasberg; *setting,* Howard Bay; *costumes*, Lucille Little; *producer*, Dwight Deere Widman; opened at the National Theatre, February 24, 1949.

CAST: John Garfield, Frank Wilson, William Terry, Leona Powers, Nancy Kelly, Reinhold Schunzel, J. Edward Bromberg, Paul McGrath, Mary Patton, Joan McCracken, Theodore Newton, John McKee.

With Reinhold Schunzel and Nancy Kelly ·

The Big Knife was a major New York theater event, bringing together several former Group Theatre members who had made their fortunes and fame in Hollywood. Advance publicity had promised an exposé of the film capital. Hollywood papers had printed bad notices even before the play opened. One noted columnist accused the star and author of "biting the hand that fed them."

The play recounts the drama of Charlie Castle, a film star who once had ideals and a sense of purpose in his life. He has watched his nobler impulses slip away in a quest for fame and riches. It was the *Golden Boy* theme in a new environment. Charlie Castle has become no more than an object, allowing his best friend to go to jail for a hit-and-run murder that was Castle's responsibility. He is unable to face his situation and lacks the will to change it; in the end, only suicide can alleviate his pain.

Harold Clurman, in his review of the play, pointed out its contradictory elements. " 'The Big Knife' is . . . a mess made by a great talent. It is neither the true story of Odets nor the clear account of a freely conceived Charlie Castle. Its subjectivity is muddled by its pretense of objectivity; its objectivity is compromised by the author's inability to distinguish between his creature and himself. 'The Big Knife,' in fact, is no

story at all, but an inchoate cry of anguish, a 'help!, help!' from the privacy of an artist's den which no one will heed because no one except the personally interested and the acute of ear will be able to identify or find reason to attend."

In attempting this half-biography, half-drama, the author and star were jumping into untried water. Most critics felt they had failed. The *Times* reviewer would not acknowledge the play's significance. "To [Odets] this Hollywood jungle is a great moral tragedy and he quotes one or two fancy phrases to prove it. But his characters are a singularly undistinguished and unattractive society of egotists, racketeers, cheats and dimwits."

But the play was hardly a conventional failure; it aroused strong sentiment both for and against. The essential problem of the play was that so much of Charlie Castle's personality and esteem had to be taken on the word of the author, never being demonstrated on stage.

Several years later the director, Robert Aldrich, commented on making the film version: "The original play had been done on Broadway with John Garfield. If you'd had an electric, charming guy like Garfield in the lead you'd have solved half the problem [of the play], but I don't think you'd ever have solved the other half."

PEER GYNT
1951

Author, Henrik Ibsen; American version by Paul Green; *director*, Lee Strasberg; *musical score*, Lan Adomian; *choreography*, Valerie Betlis; *setting and lights*, Donald Oenslager; *costumes*, Rose Bogdanoff; *Near East music*, Hillel and Aviva; *conductor*, Eugene Kusmiak; *producer*, Cheryl Crawford, with R. L. Stevens; opened at the ANTA Playhouse, January 28, 1951.

CAST: John Garfield, Mildred Dunnock, Ray Gordon, Ann Boley, John Randolph, Pearl Land, Joseph Anthony, Anne Hegira, Karl Malden, Rebecca Drake, Nehemia Persoff, Peggy Meredith, Lisa Baker, Mahon Naill, Edward Binns.

Peer Gynt was Garfield's second attempt at a nonrealistic part and his first performance in what could be called a classic play. He was unprepared for it. The production was conceived with the best of motives. It had rarely been done in this country, and it was an established production in Europe, having captivated European audiences for four decades.

In his book *Plough and Furrow*, Paul Green related the events leading to the production: "Cheryl Crawford, John Garfield, Lee Strasberg and myself were eating lunch in a midtown hotel in New York. Cheryl had called us together to discuss a project she had in mind. . . . In all our minds was the sharp memory of the valiant Group Theatre which had disbanded, and we touched on the subject more than once. . . . And then Cheryl told us that for a long time she had dreamed of doing Ibsen's 'Peer Gynt' in New York. . . 'That's a crazy play,' I spoke up. 'I've seen it done twice and it bored me stiff.' 'Still it's exactly the sort of material you're always talking about,' said Lee. 'A lot of visions, spectres, folklore, legend, dancing, music.' . . . 'It would be up to you,' said Cheryl looking at me, 'to straighten the story out, make Peer into something believable.' 'I'd like to direct it,' said Lee. 'I'd like to play Peer,' said John Garfield."

Harold Clurman said of Garfield's performance, "John Garfield, one of the few actors who has had a successful Hollywood career and still loves acting for its own sake . . . is only partly equipped for the title role. His opening scenes have a certain vigorous charm, but the later Peer, who becomes a great figure in the world arena, and then a broken old man, is at the moment definitely beyond him." Of the production, he said that it "has arresting parts . . . but little discernible unity."

The *Times* reviewer commented more succinctly, "Mr. Garfield is an admirable and likeable realistic actor. He has a magnetic personality and a warm voice; and he is winningly sincere. But he never gets Peer Gynt off the ground. His performance is literal and casual, and is completely lacking in poetic animation." Mirroring his work in *Heavenly Express*, Garfield seemed out of his milieu in this folk drama of panoramic scenes and epic stature.

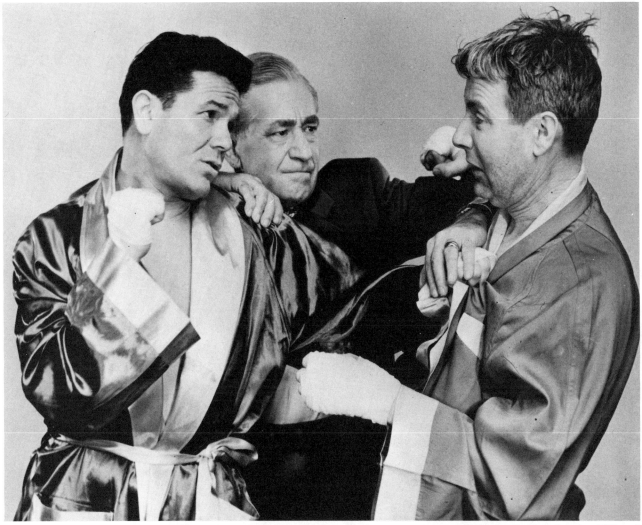

With Art Smith and Arthur O'Connell

GOLDEN BOY
1952

Author and director, Clifford Odets; *setting and lights*, Paul Morison; American National Theatre and Academy Play Series, Robert Whitehead, *managing director;* opened at the ANTA Playhouse, March 12, 1952.

CAST: John Garfield, Art Smith, Bette Grayson, William Hansen, Lee J. Cobb, Martin Greene, Joseph Wiseman, Michael Lewin, Peggy Meredith, Jack Klugman, Rudy Bond, Arthur O'Connell, Jack Warden, Sidney Kay, Gerald S. O'Laughlin, Norman Brooks, Joe Bernard, Bert Conway, Tony Kraber.

With Art Smith, Bette Grayson, Rudy Bond, and Joseph Wiseman

The return to this play for the author and star was significant. It was a central event in both their lives. Aided by a cast of former Group Theatre actors, they sought to recapture their youthful moment in the theater. It had been fifteen years since the first production, and it was something of a gamble for Odets and Garfield to undertake this revival. Times had changed, and the play might be dated. The critics generally acknowledged the power of the performance and the play. The *Times* said, " 'Golden Boy' is just as penetrating as it ever was. Perhaps the performance is even more overwhelming. For Mr. Odets has directed. . . and the acting is superb. . . . Mr. Odets never has said anything more pertinent and the Group Theatre actors have never worked at anything more valid or decisive."

For ten weeks Garfield threw himself into the role of Joe Bonaparte with his customary enthusiasm and energy. All the actors were hesitant about the performance—many of them were under the same dark political clouds as Odets and Garfield. On opening night, Roberta Garfield recalled, "Everyone was

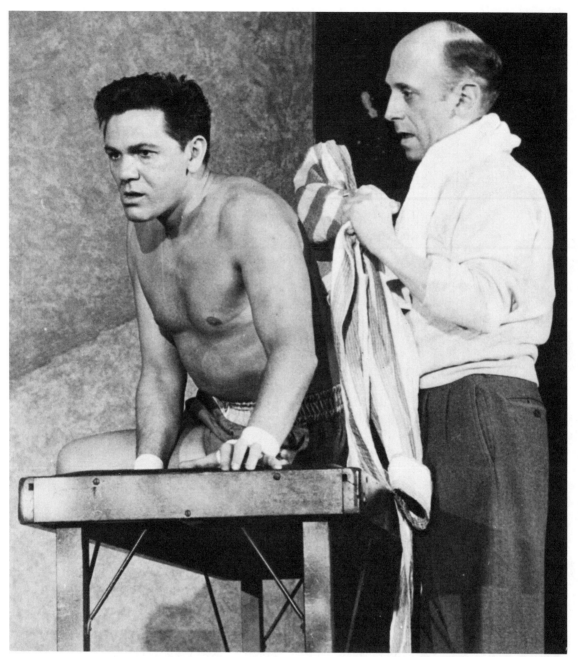

extremely nervous, even Lee Cobb, who had demonstrated Godlike stoicism in rehearsals, was shaking."

Brooks Atkinson wrote of Garfield's opening night performance, "As the prize fighter in the current performance, Mr. Garfield is giving one of his most eloquent performances, purged of the over-eager mannerisms that used to mar his acting. Apart from its fervor, his acting now is candid and forceful and more fluent than the part. Much of the writing is overwrought, but Mr. Garfield's fiery acting is wholly malleable." He had reached success in the role that was written for him.

Two months later he was dead. In an emotional letter to *The New York Times*, Clifford Odets tried to assess his friend's potential as an actor. He wrote of Garfield's ability, his enthusiasm, and his sense of purpose. Odets ended with, "I ask finally to be permitted to forget the present hushed austerity and say simply, 'Julie, dear friend, I will always love you.'"

GARFIELD AND THE BLACKLIST

There have been few detailed accounts of personal histories of blacklisted motion-picture actors, directors, or writers. What follows is an attempt to delineate the main conflicts between Garfield and congressional investigators. It is also a general view of the background and political ideas for which Garfield was held suspect.

Garfield's name appears in contemporary books on blacklisting in the motion-picture industry; however, his role in the controversy is often distorted. First, and most important, John Garfield was the best-known and probably the most successful actor to be totally blacklisted in the industry. This happened even though his name was never mentioned adversely in the testimony of any friendly or unfriendly witness nor was it ever connected officially with any subversive act, nor was any incriminating evidence put forward against him. From the time of his appearance before the House Un-American Activities Committee in April 1951 until his death, newspaper accounts presented many conflicting and confusing stories of his testimony and subsequent contacts with both the FBI and the committee. These accounts have formed the basis for many contemporary reports on Garfield.

In the largest sense, John Garfield was a minor player in the political turmoil that rocked the country in the 1950s. The motto of that period was that the current problems of the country could be solved by going back to the past—principally the years from 1932 to 1945. Those who had been out of power for almost twenty years were attempting to regain what they had lost, waging an all-out attack on whatever change or portent of change had emerged during the depression years. The thirties had symbolized the awakening of the masses to the concept of social injustice and the need for change; the fifties would symbolize the punishment of all who had held such views. Admittedly, Garfield's involvement in radical politics during this time was rare, but he was sympathetic, naïvely believing in the radical ideas of people he admired. His background contributed to his beliefs. If, in his films, he represented the class who suffered most during the depression, he was relying on personal experience.

The New York of Garfield's early years was unlike any other city in the country. For one thing, it was a city of foreigners, of first-generation Americans and their immigrant parents. At that time, it was, probably the most European of American cities. With the depression, New York became a hotbed of radical political and social activity. Communist party headquarters was on Union Square, a rallying place for demonstrations and parades (New York's equivalent of London's Hyde Park). Those who called for social and political revolution in those days were well equipped for this activity, for they were people to whom change and violence had been a way of life. They had come from a Europe only recently swept by social revolution and had undergone a tremendous upheaval in migrating to this country. The United States had promised to feed them, but it could not. "Change the system!" they shouted.

To be a young man in the thirties was to know material deprivation but also to feel as if one were in the middle of a storm. It was a time when slogans, parades, and mass meetings served to assuage people's fear. The proletarian novel appeared. The radical journal *New Masses* printed stories and articles by the best writers of the day, and soon the theater, too, would lend its voice to revolution. Starting out in the thirties, as Alfred Kazin puts it, meant being "engulfed by Socialists who were Norman Thomas Socialists, old-line Social Democrats, Austro-Marxists; Communists who were Stalinist centrists, Trotskyite leftists, Lovestoneite right-wingers, Musteites and Fieldites; Zionists who were Progressive Labor Zionists, left Socialist Zionists, and Religious Zionists—all the most accomplished philosophers ever born to the New York streets, tireless virtuosi who threw radical argument at each other morning, noon and night. . . . "

This was the ideological world in which Garfield was nurtured. It is obvious that the people involved ran the gamut from serious-minded revolutionaries to faddists and hangers-on. But, as would often be true in the next decades, some of the best writing, thinking, and art came from these embroiled men and women of the political left in New York.

The thirties, in fact, never really faded from the consciousness of Americans who felt hemmed in and threatened by this "foreign" influence. With the end of World War II, interest in the depression years became an obsession linked to tales of treason, sabotage, and betrayal. And all this fed on instilled paronoid feelings left over from the war years.

The House Un-American Activities Committee's involvement in Hollywood has been described before in greater detail. The general facts are that in 1947 HUAC stated its desire to investigate alleged communist activities in the motion-picture industry. It would subpoena several dozen people, from executives to directors, writers, and actors. In protest, numbers of industry workers organized the Committee for the First Amendment to combat what they termed unjust and illegal questioning of one's political beliefs. But the Committee for the First Amendment dissolved when industry executives failed to support it. Contrary to their earlier vote of approval, the executives let it be known that any employee who refused to answer all questions put by congressional investigators would be unwelcome at the studios. The first group to refuse to answer questions, the so-called Hollywood Ten, were cited for contempt and served jail sentences. By 1949 the picture in Hollywood was grim.

Garfield was a likely choice for committee investigation; his New York background and work with the Group Theatre were well-known, and Roberta Garfield, his wife, had been an active supporter of left-wing causes. His appearance before the committee in April 1951 was termed friendly, but he was determined not to name anyone as a Communist. He would not even name publicly known Communists, those who made no secret of their affiliation. Garfield had somehow worked out a staunch adherence to a code that would not allow him to betray any friend.

It should be obvious from his testimony that he was not politically adept; his beliefs were general and determined by personal loyalty, and he lacked the ability to parry the congressional questioners or to castigate them. The course he chose was to deny all allegations and avoid naming names; this did not satisfy the committee. Representative Moulder seems to have been Garfield's only ally, and his questions suggest that he had been won over prior to the actual hearing. One of the confusing aspects to Garfield's appearance in Washington was the celebrity treatment he received by the very people who would attack him in the hearing room.

The committee investigators had no practical evidence to present; they had only vague newspaper clippings and second-hand gossip. His Group Theatre activities and his wife's political affiliations could not be used against him. But the committee did have one weapon to wield—any shadow of suspicion would effectively stop his career. It was a weapon they did not have to use directly; they simply stated their dissatisfaction. The one statement by Garfield that they tried to contradict concerned his never having known a Communist. An attempt was made by the FBI to secure witnesses who would acknowledge Garfield's having known Communists and thus make his statement perjurious. In the year after his testimony all such attempts failed, but in the meantime he was unemployable.

Lack of work was debilitating to him. Eventually he sought help to clear himself of the still undocumented charges. The scenario written for him would have been particularly public—a full confession of past misdeeds in the form of an exposé article written for one of the popular magazines, entitled "I Was a Sucker for a Left Hook." Then, in a second appearance before the committee, he would name names. The old ritual would be followed.

His dilemma was that in order to work he had to follow this prepared script. The day after his death a number of anti-Communist newspaper columnists printed stories that Garfield had been on the verge of a full confession; one columnist put the disclosure in the form of a conversation he said he'd had with the actor a few hours before he died. In retrospect, however, it is apparent that those who publicized this undocumented confession had a vested interest in anti-Communist disclosures. Certainly they were not concerned with exposing the pressure tactics that were used to obtain confessions. Many of these people were in the business of "exposing Reds."

It is still a fact that Garfield's name does not appear on any document disavowing his past, and he made no public confession or second appearance before the HUAC. Even in his last hours, he was still resisting that final act of capitulation. A contemporary who shared Garfield's experience with the Blacklist commented that he "was not protecting himself, but old friends whose names had been mentioned dozens of times. He wasn't keeping a secret. Just an idea of himself. That he collapsed before it did is a victory."

Excerpts from Testimony before the House

The following is the testimony of John Garfield before the House Un-American Activities Committee on April 23, 1951. He was accompanied by his counsel, Louis Nizer and Sidney Davis. The text is a selection of questions and answers.

MR. TAVENNER: Mr. Garfield. after you were served with a subpoena to appear before this committee as a witness, the New York Times carried a statement attributed to you which is as follows:

> I have always hated communism. It is a tyranny which threatens our country and the peace of the world. Of course, then, I have never been a member of the Communist Party or a sympathizer with any of its doctrines. I wil be pleased to cooperate with the committee.

MR. GARFIELD: Absolutely.

MR. TAVENNER: Is it a fact that you have always hated communism, as stated in that news release?

MR. GARFIELD: Absolutely, yes.

MR. TAVENNER: Are you of the opinion and belief that communism is a tyranny which threatens our country and the peace of the world?

MR. GARFIELD: I believe so. I think it is a subversive movement and is a tyranny and is a dictatorship and is against democracy.

MR. TAVENNER: Have you ever been a member of the Communist Party.

MR. GARFIELD: I have never been a member of the Community Party.

MR. TAVENNER: If you are willing to cooperate with the committee, as stated in this news release, in its endeavor to ascertain the extent of communist infiltration into the entertainment field, particularly into the motion picture industry, it will be necessary to ask you questions relating to your knowledge of communist activities in that field, and especially about your own conduct in connection with organizations to which you have belonged and as to experiences which you have had. I understand you are willing to cooperate with the committee?

MR. GARFIELD: Mr. Tavenner, I will answer any question you put to me. . . .

MR. TAVENNER: While you were a member of the Group Theatre, did anything occur to lead you to believe that there was communist activity within the Group in the form of an effort to influence its action or the way in which it operated?

MR. GARFIELD: You mean in the actual functioning of the organization or the plays that were done?

MR. TAVENNER: In the functioning of the organization or the adoption of the policies which it followed.

MR. GARFIELD: I don't think so. As I said, it was purely run on an artistic basis. It was not a political organization. Of course the actors on Broadway used to call us peculiar because we didn't accept employment on the outside, and took much less money than we usually would get, because we wanted to work together. And we worked in a certain way. We had a technical craft and worked in a certain way, and they thought that was kind of strange.

MR. TAVENNER: Did you hold camps out in the State of New York in a place named Ellenville?

MR. GARFIELD: Oh, yes. We didn't have camps. I can explain that. We went out every summer, with our children, families, to rehearse the next season's play. We went to Ellenville and took an old hotel, and all the people lived in the hotel through the summer, to rehearse the play.

MR. TAVENNER: Do you recall any occasions when at those camps people were brought in who attacked the principles of our form of government?

MR. GARFIELD: I do not, sir, I do recall, however, that one of the directors, or two, I am not just clear, had just come from Moscow where they had seen the Moscow Art Theater, and they talked about that. That is my best recollection of that. It is pretty long ago. . . .

MR. TAVENNER: Did you at any time make any contributions to a publication known as the New Masses, and I call your attention particularly to the year 1945 when a person by the name of Doretta Tarmon, T-a-r-m-o-n, was active in securing donations?

MR. GARFIELD: And she claimed she got money from me?

MR. TAVENNER: I am asking if you did make contributions to it?

MR. GARFIELD: I don't know this person.

MR. TAVENNER: You do not?

MR. GARFIELD: No.

MR. TAVENNER: Well, did you make contributions to the New Masses through any other person?

MR. GARFIELD: I might have possibly subscribed to it from a dramatic, literary point of view, but I never made any contributions.

MR. TAVENNER: The New Masses is known as a communist publication. There were other publications.

MR. GARFIELD: For instance, I subscribe to the Christian Science Monitor and Time Magazine.

MR. TAVENNER: But what I am asking is whether you took part in any benefit or made any contributions—I am not talking about subscribing to the publication, but made a contribution to the People's World, the Daily Worker, and those papers?

MR. GARFIELD: No, sir. . . .

MR. TAVENNER: As an actor it was necessary for you to become a member of the Actors' Guild, was it not?

MR. GARFIELD: Yes, sir.

MR. TAVENNER: In 1945, during the period of the strike in the moving picture industry, the Communist Party is alleged to have been interested in influencing various groups in connection with that strike. Do you have any knowledge on your own part regarding that effort?

MR. GARFIELD: Well, I have no knowledge of what the

Un-American Activities Committee

Communist Party was doing because I had no association with anybody like that, but I was on the executive board of the Screen Actors' Guild for 6 years, and during the period of this strike, and I know pretty well what went on in terms of the strike, in terms of the guild's position, and in terms of the general atmosphere at that time. . . .

MR. TAVENNER: During the period in which the Communist Party was interesting itself in that particular strike movement, was there any time when your views coincided with the Communist Party views and aims in connection with that strike, or were they at all times divergent?

MR. GARFIELD: I would say at most times they were divergent, but I didn't know their point of view. Once I remember a meeting of about 150 actors at a private home which I heard about and went to. As a matter of fact, Ronald Reagan was there, and when he saw me he was surprised, and when I saw him I was surprised, and we reported this at a meeting, that there were special meetings being held. The membership of the Screen Actors' Guild voted 98.9 percent against supporting this strike, eventually.

MR. TAVENNER: Are you still a member of the guild?

MR. GARFIELD: I am not a member of the executive board, but I am a member of the Screen Actors' Guild; yes, sir.

MR. TAVENNER: During the period of this controversy, were you able to identify any person who, from their statements to you or from other evidence that would satisfy you, were members of the Communist Party, in connection with the activities on this problem?

MR. GARFIELD: Well, they were in favor, for instance, of the position of the CSU, which we weren't.

MR. VELDE: I don't think you have answered the question that counsel asked you. He asked if you knew of any Communist Party members?

MR. GARFIELD: Officially, do you mean?

MR. TAVENNER: Either from statements they made to you or from what you learned about them?

MR. GARFIELD: No, sir. . . .

MR. TAVENNER: Mr. Garfield, the committee is in possession of considerable information relating to various Communist front organizations with which you are alleged to have affiliated in one way or another, or sponsored, and I would like to ask you some questions about those. . . .

MR. TAVENNER: Do you recall on July 20, 1944 that the Joint Anti-Fascist Refugee Committee sponsored what was called a free people's dinner at the Beverly Hills Hotel to raise funds for the transportation of anti-Axis leaders out of France?

MR. GARFIELD: If it was during the war, it is possible I might have been at this meeting, but I don't specifically remember that function.

MR. TAVENNER: You don't remember whether you were a sponsor of it or not?

MR. GARFIELD: No, sir. You know, I would like to point

out, Mr. Tavenner, what a difficult and tough situation a guy like me is in, because I get a million requests all the time from various organizations, some very worthy ones, and I would like to point out to the committee an example of what happened to me, because, I am in this situation where I am in the public eye and people think "He is a nice guy; maybe he will do it for us; why not do it," and so forth. I have a letter from the National Citizens Political Action Committee dated August 7, 1945, in which it is stated,

> The executive board invites you to serve on this general council because of your continued interest in our organization. Meetings will not be called frequently so that the time demand will not be too great.

I would like to point out particularly this last paragraph.

> We sincerely hope that you will join us in the work of our important organization. We would appreciate knowing your wishes in this matter. If we receive no reply from you by Friday, August 17, we will consider your position as accepting membership on our general council.

I answered "No" but it is just possible that things like this would come to me and I would throw it away in a wastebasket, and 3 months from now I would be on this committee.

MR. JACKSON: Mr. Chairman, may I just suggest—

MR. WOOD: Mr. Jackson.

MR. JACKSON: That isn't every other person in the motion picture industry in precisely the same position?

MR. GARFIELD: Pretty much so; yes.

MR. JACKSON: And isn't it true there are literally hundreds of people in the industry whose actions have never made them suspect?

MR. GARFIELD: Possibly, but I have always been an outstanding liberal.

MR. VELDE: You say you are an outstanding liberal?

MR. GARFIELD: That is what they said.

MR. VELDE: You mentioned a while ago that the Communist Party didn't trust you.

MR. GARFIELD: They don't trust liberals.

MR. POTTER: Many times they use liberals.

MR. GARFIELD: They try; yes, sir.

MR. JACKSON: I would say Alger Hiss was known as a very outstanding liberal. Certainly he gained some element of approval and acceptance by the Communist Party.

MR. KEARNEY: And also by the Government of the United States. . . .

MR. TAVENNER: The New York Times of March 3, 1945, contained an advertisement paid for by the Veterans of the Abraham Lincoln Brigade advocating a break with Franco Spain. Among those listed as sponsoring the Veterans of the Abraham Lincoln Brigade is your name.

MR. GARFIELD: Again let me say to the committee and to you that I was for Spain because I felt it was a

FBI Told Of Reds by Garfield

(Photos on Pages 10 and 11.)

Actor John Garfield, 39, was trying to make a Saturday deadline with an expose of Communists when death suddenly closed his turbulent career.

This was revealed today after Garfield was found dead of a heart attack in the apartment of a blond former actress, Iris Whitney, 36, at 3 Gramercy Park West.

The stage and screen "Golden Boy," whose early struggles admittedly made him a sucker for a Left hook, had at least two movie offers—if he cleared a cloud of suspicion.

IGNORED BY HOLLYWOOD.

He had been ignored by Hollywood studios for 18 months since his doubtful performance when he told the House Un-American Activities Committee he didn't know any Communists.

He needed work. He approached a group of anti-Communists for advice on clearing himself. He was told to tell the truth—and name names of every Communist he knew.

Garfield was to have turned in his statement by Saturday—but death's deadline came first. His story, however, was in the hands of Federal authorities since he had visited the FBI.

Dr. Thomas Gonzales, Chief Medical Examiner, said he saw no reason for ordering an autopsy because "there was absolutely no question but that death was due to a heart attack."

The actor's body, found at 10 a.m. yesterday in a bed at Miss

Continued on Page 11, Column 4.

John Garfield Swears He Was Never a Red

Offers Answer To Any Question

By the United Press.

WASHINGTON, April 23.— Movie star John Garfield told the House Un-American Activities Committee today "I have never been a member of the Communist party" and will answer "any question you put to me."

The 38-year-old actor, the first witness following a six-day recess, told the committee:

"I believe communism is a tyranny, a dictatorship, and is against democracy."

Fifth Friendly Witness.

Mr. Garfield's offer of full cooperation made him the fifth "friendly" witness in the current investigation, but the first to say he was never a Communist.

Four previous witnesses said they were one-time Hollywood Communists. They were stars Larry Parks and Sterling Hayden, writer Richard J. Collins and Mrs. Meta Reis Rosenberg, former assistant story editor of Paramount Studios.

Academy award actor Jose Ferrer is expected to be called to the witness stand later this week.

Both Mr. Garfield and Mr. Ferrer issued statements earlier denying they were ever Communists and offering to co-operate with the committee.

Not Called Reds.

Nobody had called them Communists in the current hearings. However, the committee reported recently that Mr. Ferrer was affiliated with "five to 10" organizations which had been cited as subversive and had backed Communist election candidates.

Acme Telephoto.
Screen actor John Garfield testifying in Washington today.

Mr. Garfield was born in New York and was a successful stage actor before switching to films in 1943. The Puerto-Rican-born Ferrer, 39, was known mainly for his stage roles before he won an Oscar for his 1950 performance of "Cyrano de Bergerac."

democratically elected government. I was against the Communists in there as much as I was against the Fascists in there. That was my position and has always been my position. I was and still am against the Communists and against the Fascists. However, on this particular point that you mention, I have no knowledge of ever giving permission to them to use my name. The only organization that I worked with about Spain was an organization called the Theater Arts Committee.

MR. TAVENNER: Were you a member of or associated with Veterans of the Abraham Lincoln Brigade?

MR. GARFIELD: No, sir.

MR. TAVENNER: Or with the Friends of the Abraham Lincoln Brigade?

MR. GARFIELD: No, sir.

MR. TAVENNER: Did you know at the time that the Abraham Lincoln Brigade was a Communist sponsored group?

MR. GARFIELD: No, sir; I didn't know it. Had I known it—although I don't remember having sponsored this particular event—I would have had nothing to do with it. But I still feel the same way about Spain.

MR. VELDE: You had no reason to believe that group was communist sponsored?

MR. GARFIELD: No, sir.

MR. TAVENNER: You mentioned earlier you were a member of the Committee for the First Amendment?

MR. GARFIELD: Yes, sir. . . .

MR. POTTER: You stated you wanted to make sure there were no communists identified with this movement, Committee for the First Amendment. You must have known of a certain movement, or of certain communist activity, in Hollywood, or you would not have been suspicious of it?

MR. GARFIELD: That was because of the hearing, you know.

MR. POTTER: If you were so cautious as to make sure no communist was identified with your group, certainly you knew of communist activity in Hollywood or you would not have been so cautious?

MR. GARFIED: No, not necessarily; not necessarily.

MR. POTTER: All right.

MR. GARFIELD: We had, as a matter of fact, on that committee, very strong liberals and very strong conservatives.

MR. POTTER: You don't believe there were any communists identified with the group?

MR. GARFIEID: I made the point very clear, "If we are going to fight on that issue, we must be sure there is nobody in the organization with a left tinge." If you will look at the list of people who came here in 1947, the list will speak for itself, I am sure.

MR. POTTER: That was in protest to the hearings in 1947?

MR. GARFIELD: Exactly.

MR. POTTER: If I remember, at that time 10 Hollywood people were cited for contempt who refused to cooperate with the committee, and some of those, I am sure,

were known communists.

MR. GARFIELD: But they were not on the Committee for the First Amendment. We were fighting on general principles. It had nothing to do with these people. That is the whole point. It has nothing to do with these individuals, believe me. It had to do with the two basic principles. It had nothing to do with the indivduals.

MR. WOOD: What you mean is that that was your conception of it?

MR. GARFIELD: Yes. As I have said, I wasn't in on the organization of it. I wasn't in California. Some 2 or 3 months later I did a play, Skipper Next to God, and the Daily Worker panned me and said I was a little punch-drunk for playing in a religious play like Skipper Next to God.

MR. VELDE: How did you know about the Daily Worker saying that?

MR. GARFIELD: I look in all papers and try to find out all information about myself.

MR. VELDE: I was interested in how you happened to see it.

MR. GARFIELD: Would you like to see the copy?

MR. VELDE: No. I have seen many copies of the Daily Worker. I asked how you happened to look at the Daily Worker.

MR. GARFIELD: They review all plays.

MR. VELDE: There is nothing sinister in my question.

MR. GARFIELD: Most actors, if they are actors at all; like to see all the reviews, regardless of what paper publishes them. That was a review of a play I was in.

MR. VELDE: You still haven't answered my question, Mr. Garfield. How did you happen to get hold of a copy of the Daily Worker?

MR. GARFIELD: It was a review in the Daily Worker.

MR. VELDE: I realize that. Do you remember where you obtained the copy?

MR. GARFIELD: Yes. I got a copy by buying a copy. They have a dramatic critic and they review plays just like the New York Times, or the Herald Tribune.

MR. MOULDER: We subscribe to the Daily Worker here.

MR. JACKSON: And the witness should know that this committee also shared the criticism of the Daily Worker. . . .

MR. WOOD: You have indicated some knowledge of the Communist Party at that time and its activities. How could you possibly know anything about the activities of the Communist Party if you didn't know who its members were?

MR. GARFIELD: I had no knowledge who its members were, and didn't know all its workings.

MR. WOOD: How could you formulate an opinion?

MR. GARFIELD: Mr. Potter asked me when I changed.

MR. WOOD: You can't change your position on an organization that you don't know anything about, can you?

MR. GARFIELD: I felt this way: I was for Wallace up until the time he ran on a ticket that I thought was being captured by a small group of people in general. I didn't know the people specifically. I felt he was being captured.

MR. WOOD: Did I understand you to say you thought Wallace was being captured by people who were members of the Communist Party?

MR. GARFIELD: Yes.

MR. WOOD: How did you know that?

MR. GARFIELD: That was public knowledge. I had no other information except that.

MR. WOOD: It is my understanding you didn't know any of the people who formed the group that took him over?

MR. GARFIELD: Who captured him?

MR. WOOD: Yes.

MR. GARFIELD: No.

MR. WOOD: You still think it was a communist group?

MR. GARFIELD: Yes.

MR. WOOD: And you still say you didn't know a single one of those?

MR. GARFIELD: Except from the newspapers. But that is when I broke away.

MR. WOOD: You broke away from what?

MR. GARFIELD: From the Progressive Party.

MR. WOOD: You had been affiliated with the Progressive Party?

MR. GARFIELD: I was not a member of it. The only party I was ever a member of was the Democratic Party, but I contributed money to the Progressive Citizens of America because they were an arm of the Democratic Party on some issues. For instance, they backed Mrs. Douglas in California. I supported her.

MR. WOOD: Let me ask you categorically, have you any knowledge of the identity of a single individual who was a member of the Communist Party during the time you were in Hollywood?

MR. GARFIELD: No, sir.

MR. MOULDER: Mr. Chairman?

MR. WOODS Mr. Moulder.

MR. MOULDER: As I understand, you formed your opinion not by any personal knowledge of or association with any member of the Communist Party, but like all of us, you formulated your opinion from general information that was disseminated?

MR. GARFIELD: Exactly, Mr. Congressman. . . .

MR. TAVENNER: Mr. Garfield, there has been information regarding a trip you made to a Russian ship on the west coast. Is there any significance to that?

MR. GARFIELD: I would like to tell the committee the facts on that. In 1945 or 1946 the State Department invited Constantine Semenov to come to the United States at their expense. Mr. Semenov was shown around the various studios and was entertained at Robert Montgomery's house and at the homes of many other people. We made the gesture of friendly relationship with him, cultural exchange. I met Mr. Semenov the first time in Hollywood, and he invited us to come and have a drink with him on a Russian ship in San Pedro. We went and had a drink. The press

was there. We invited the press in. A State Department official was there who was the interpreter. That is the first and last time I saw Mr. Semenov.

MR. MOULDER: What was the date of that?

MR. GARFIELD: 1945 or 1946. It was the tag end of the war.

MR. TAVENNER: Was there any other occasion when you visited a Russian ship?

MR. GARFIELD: No.

MR. TAVENNER: Do you recall on one occasion there was shown a Russian film, The Bear?

MR. GARFIELD: The Bear was written by Anton Chekhov in 1870. It was the story of a man who comes to woo a widow, and it is kind of amusing, funny. They showed that picture. It is a one-act picture. This was on this particular occasion.

MR. TAVENNER: This same occasion?

MR. GARFIELD: Yes. Somebody said we were shown a propaganda film called The Bear. You can go to any public library and read The Bear and you will see it has no such indication of any kind.

MR. WALTER: It is a very old story?

MR. GARFIELD: That is right.

MR. TAVENNER: I believe your name appears on a brief amicus curiae filed in the case of the Hollywood Ten before the Supreme Court?

MR. GARFIELD: Yes.

MR. TAVENNER: I believe the brief was originally filed under the name of Alexander Meiklejohn. M-e-i-k-l-e-j-o-h-n. Will you tell us the circumstances under which you signed the brief?

MR GARFIELD: Well, I was asked to sign it, and I said I wouldn't sign unless many other people signed it who were not in any way leftist, because I felt that I wouldn't want to lend my name to anything like that unless other people in the industry did; and they did.

MR. TAVENNER: How were arrangements made for you to join in?

MR. GARFIELD: It was not joining in. Somebody approached me and asked if I would be a nice guy and do it. I said I wouldn't unless some other people did. They said, "All right, go get other people." I thought I was being on the court's side when I signed this document, a friend of the court. I thought it was important that a man is never guilty until proven so, and it was on that principle and that alone that I signed the document, but I certainly was not the only one.

MR. WOOD: Do you recall who first approached you on that subject?

MR. GARFIELD: Well, as I explained to Mr. Russell or Mr. Wheeler—

MR. WOOD: We were not there at the time.

MR. GARFIELD: I vaguely remember being approached at the Beverly Hills Tennis Club

MR. WOOD: And you can't recall who brought the conversation up?

MR. GARFIELD: They asked if it wasn't a person named

Wilner, and I said I wasn't sure if it was or wasn't. But this particular person, Mr. Chairman, was a member of that club, so it is possible he was the one that asked me. I am not sure on that.

MR. TAVENNER: Do you remember whether it was a man or a woman?

MR. GARFIELD: I can't remember if it was a man or a woman, but it is possible it might have been a woman. I can't honestly remember. But I know that is where I was asked, at the Beverly Hills Tennis Club.

MR. WOOD: Prior to that time had you ever signed a brief in the Supreme Court in any case?

MR. GARFIELD: No.

MR. WOOD: This was the only brief you had signed in the Supreme Court in any case?

MR. GARFIELD: Yes, Mr. Chairman.

MR. WOOD: And you are unable, notwithstanding that was an event that occurred only once in your life, to give the committee the identity of the person who discussed it with you?

MR. GARFIELD: I would if I remembered. I have a vague recollection that this Wilner person approached me. I am not sure. But I know I was approached at this tennis club.

MR. WOOD: The reason I asked that question, you have been rather positive in some of the things you have been asked about, that you not only did not sign a petition to join certain organizations but that you wouldn't do so, and here is an event it seems to me would be rather important in a man's life—

MR. GARFIELD: I signed this.

MR. WOOD: But would you have signed it if just anybody had walked up and asked you to?

MR. GARFIELD: Not if it was any stranger; no.

MR. WOOD: And you can't give the committee any further identification of the person who approached you on that subject than what you have given?

MR. GARFIELD: I tried to recall, as I said. If I knew it I would really gladly tell it, but I know I was approached at the Beverly Hills Tennis Club.

MR. WOOD: All right . . . .

MR. MOULDER: First I want to compliment the witness upon his statement that he has always been against communism, that it is a tyranny which threatens our country and the peace of the world. And I feel morally inclined to express my opinion that nothing has been presented by the committee which associates you with the Communist Party. Everyone who is brought before this committee is not necessarily accused of being a communist, but is brought here to give such information as he may have on communist activities or subversive activities. And I don't think anybody who is a liberal should be condemned in the slightest degree. Jefferson was a liberal, and so was Lincoln.

MR. GARFIELD: Thank you. . . .

MR. VELDE: Do you want to go on record as saying you had no knowledge whatsoever of any Communist Party movement in Hollywood until the time you broke with the Wallace Party?

MR. GARFIELD: Absolutely and positively. . . .

MR. JACKSON: Mr. Garfield, I am still afraid that I am not entirely convinced of the entire accuracy and entire cooperation you are giving this committee. It is your contention you did not know, during the time you were in New York affiliated with the Group Theatre, which for all its artistry was pretty well shot through with the philosophy of communism—

MR. GARFIELD: That is not true.

MR. JACKSON: That is a matter of opinion. You contend during all that time in New York you did not know a communist?

MR. GARFIELD: That is right.

MR. JACKSON: And you contend that during the 7½ years or more that you were in Hollywood and in close contact with a situation in which a number of communist cells were operating on a week-to-week basis, with electricians, actors, and every class represented, that during the entire period of time you were in Hollywood you did not know of your own personal knowledge a member of the Communist Party?

MR. GARFIELD: That is absolutely correct, because I was not a party member or associated in any shape, way or form.

MR. JACKSON: During that period it might interest you to know attempts were made to recruit me into the Communist Party and I was making $32.50 a week.

MR. GARFIELD: They certainly stayed away from me, sir.

MR. JACKSON: Perhaps I looked like better material. This picture, He Ran All the Way—who produced it?

MR. GARFIELD: I did.

MR. JACKSON: You produced it?

MR. GARFIELD: I didn't have any screen credit for producing it, but I always work as a coproducer.

MR. JACKSON: The script was by whom?

MR. GARFIELD: Guy Endore and Hugo Butler.

MR. JACKSON: Who directed it?

MR. GARFIELD: Jack Berry.

MR. JACKSON: You have never been approached at any time to join the Communist Party?

MR. GARFIELD: Never.

MR. JACKSON: Nor have you been approached to assist at Communist Party functions or functions of Communist-front organizations when you knew they were front organizations?

MR. GARFIELD: That is right, Mr. Jackson. I might say, if at any time that had happened, I would have run like hell.

MR. JACKSON: I must say. Mr. Chairman, in conclusion, that I am still not satisfied. . . .

MR. POTTER: Mr. Garfield, you told the committee of

John Garfield, shown testifying before House Un-American probers last year, talked to the Mirror's Victor Riesel shortly before actor's death. He gave Riesel details of statement he had just finished writing, telling how Reds trapped actors.

(AP Photo)

Garfield Bared Traps by Reds

By VICTOR RIESEL

A few hours before his death, actor John Garfield completed a full statement describing how Hollywood Communists adroitly wove a web around him and other emotional and sentimental actors who sought to become crusaders but who didn't have the time to check the camouflaged "causes" to which they gave their support.

"Julie" Garfield talked to me shortly before he died. He made an appointment to come up and see me and have a drink and give me the details of the statement he had just finished. He gave me a synopsis of how his 20 years in Hollywood had been a constant nightmare, how strangers went up to him on the street and warned him to keep quiet, of the phone calls he got in the dead of night calling him a "rat" for blowing the whistle on the Reds who had all but ruined his life and his career.

The statement was to have modified his testimony last year before the House Un-American Activities Committee, when he denied he knew any Communists. He was to admit he worked closely with Reds and carried out their orders.

The Reds came under different guises: Businessmen, publicists, secretaries; tennis club friends and do gooders would rush him into a corner and quickly deliver the pitch. It was a wonderful cause, they said, and John Gar-

Continued on Page 30

your activities in the liberal fields of endeavor. Other witnesses before the committee who have been so-called liberals have pointed out that the communists have endeavored to recruit them, because at many points they use many activities to recruit so-called liberals into the party. In answer to a question by Mr. Jackson you stated you have never been recruited or approached to be recruited?

MR. GARFIELD: That is true. No one has ever—

MR. POTTER: No one has ever approached you to join the Communist Party?

MR. GARFIELD: That is true, Mr. Potter. I was never approached. . . .

MR. POTTER: Apparently, the committee has received not only testimony but certain evidence from publications of alleged membership that you had that you now deny. Did you have knowledge of articles, for example, which appeared in the Daily Worker, which lauded you for such and such activities?

MR. GARFIELD: I also have proof they panned me. I know the organizations I am a member of: YMCA, Hoyle Club, Democratic Club, B'nai B'rith.

MR. POTTER: You don't appear to be a naive man.

MR. GARFIELD: I am not, I don't think.

MR. POTTER: It is difficult to understand. If I got lauded in the Daily Worker, I would begin to suspect—

MR. GARFIELD: You mean anybody mentioned in the Daily Worker is suspect?

MR. POTTERS I would try to find out what they were up to.

MR. GARFIELD: Senator Taft was praised by the Daily Worker for his refusal to send troops to Europe. Does that mean he is on their team, so to speak?

MR. POTTER: I think the reference to Senator Taft was a little different from the references I am speaking of here, and I am sure the Daily Worker has not made a constant effort to laud the Senator. I am not asking about Senator Taft's activities. But it seems incredible that you could be identified with movements which, looking back now, the communists have used, without suspecting it until the Wallace break.

MR. GARFIELD: I was not identified with these people. I was never active in these organizations, Mr. Potter.

MR. POTTER: Are you a joiner by nature?

MR. GARFIELD: No; I am not a joiner by nature; I am not.

MR. POTTER: Do you use any precautions to protect your name, to keep people from using your name when you don't want them to use it?

MR. GARFIELD: How can you protect it when somebody writes you a letter and says "If you don't answer in a week we will consider you a member"?

MR. POTTER: I would answer it right away if I didn't want them to use my name; and, if they did, I would take every legal means available.

MR. GARFIELD: I did, sir. I have not taken legal means, but I intend to.

MR. POTTER: You intend to. That is all.

MR. WOOD: Mr. Moulder, did you have additional questions?

MR. MOULDER: No questions; but, to answer Mr. Jackson's statement, I am convinced that no man should be convicted nor condemned on pure hearsay, rumor or gossip. I sympathize with your position. Being one of the outstanding actors in this country, naturally you are going to be the subject of such rumor and gossip. I don't think any man should be criticized because he is a liberal Republican or a liberal Democrat. The statement I made to you reminds me of an experience in my last campaign when my opponent accused me of being a "pink."

MR. JACKSON: The Democrats made similar charges.

MR. MOULDER: He also accused me of making statements against this committee which was not true. I wish to reiterate my statement that your appearance before this committee does not of itself mean you are accused of being a communist. I am clearly convinced from all the testimony adduced that you were never associated with the Communist Party or any Communist activity or subversive activity, and that you are a loyal American; and I compliment you on your vigilant fight against communism and your cooperation with this committee.

MR. JACKSON: Mr. Chairman, so long as my name has been brought into this discussion, I would like to say I do not believe any man is guilty by association or anything of that sort. I am sure the gentleman from Missouri had no intention of accusing me of anything like that. I do say that, for one who is as intelligent as this witness has proven himself to be, it shows a naive or unintelligent approach to this problem for him to have lived with this activity 10, 11, or 15 years and not know more about it than this witness knows.

MR. GARFIELD: Mr. Jackson, may I answer that? I went overseas twice. I was too busy with war work. I am now conscious of what you are saying, more conscious than I ever was, but in that time I was more conscious of my bigger duty, which was to my country, and where I as an artist could contribute.

MR. JACKSON: Unfortunately, the work in which you were engaged became more suspect than the work of those overseas. . . .

MR. MOULDER: The statement was made that you belonged to organizations the purpose of which was the overthrow of our Government by force and violence. As I understand your testimony, you have emphatically denied that you belonged to such organizations?

MR. GARFIELD: Yes, sir. Thank you.

MR. JACKSON: Actors' Laboratory is listed as a subversive organization.

MR. GARFIELD: I was never a member of that organization.

MR. JACKSON: The witness appeared on behalf of Actors' Laboratory. I would correct my statement from "membership in" to "activity on behalf of" organizations that have been cited as subversive.

MR. GARFIELD: When I was originally requested to appear before the committee, I said that I would answer all questions fully and without any reservations and that is what I have done. I have nothing to be ashamed of and nothing to hide. My life is an open book. I was glad to appear before you and talk with you. I am no Red. I am no "pink." I am no fellow traveler. I am a Democrat by politics, a liberal by inclination, and a loyal citizen of this country by every act of my life.

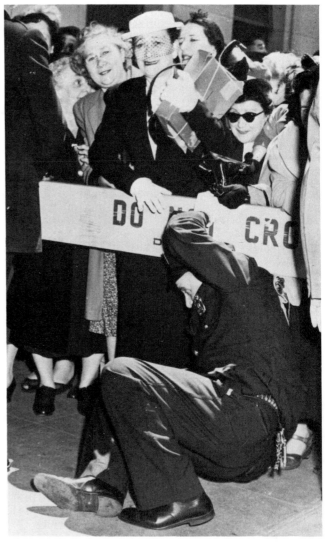

A near-riot at the funeral chapel

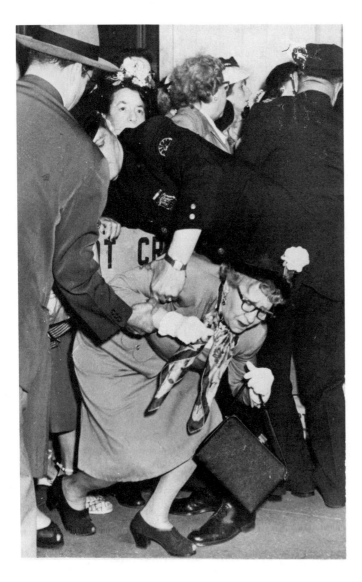

10,000 Jam Street At Garfield Rites

While a crowd of 10,000—mostly women—jammed the street outside and shoved against police barricades, funeral services for John Garfield, famed for his 'tough guy' Hollywood roles, were held yesterday by a quiet-spoken rabbi in a dimly lighted funeral chapel.

After the 25-minute service, eight minutes of which were devoted to a eulogy, the body was carried through lines of police, who pushed back the curious, and taken to

Hushed crowd of mourners watches pallbearers carry casket containing the body of John Garfield from Riverside Funeral Chapel, 76th St. and Amsterdam Ave. (Other photos on Page 1)

(Mirror Photo)

Westchester Hills Cemetery at Hastings-on-Hudson, N. Y., for burial.

Garfield, 39, died Wednesday of a heart attack in the apartment of actress Iris Whitney.

Fifty police, joined by five radio cars which stood bumper to bumper across the intersection, handled the thousands of curious outside the Riverside Funeral Chapel at 76th St. and Amsterdam Ave. Morton Rosenthal, president of the chapel, said the turnout was the greatest in the history of that institution, far eclipsing the previous high mark set at the funeral for band leader Ben Bernie.

Inside, among many friends from the entertainment world, were such stars as Milton Berle, Jose Ferrer, Burgess Meredith, Luther Adler, Lee Cobb, Zero Mostel, Betty Grayson who was Garfield's leading lady in the recent revival of "Golden Boy," and Hollywood producer Joseph Mankiewicz.

The late actor's two children, David, 9, and Julie, 6, wept as Rabbi Louis I. Newman of Temple Rodeph Soholom spoke, but his wife, Roberta, retained her composure.

In his eulogy, Newman de-

Truman Signs Bills Boosting Disabled Vets' Pensions

WASHINGTON, May 23 (AP).—PRESIDENT Truman today signed two bills increasing pensions to disabled veterans. They are expected ultimately to cost the government more than $400,000,000 a year.

Truman said he approved the measures "with great reluctance."

scribed Garfield as "a child of the city; a child of his age; a son of our epoch" and made an oblique reference to the actor's recent trouble over affiliation with Red groups.

"He came to know that life can grow cruel indeed," the rabbi said. "He strove to maintain his integrity and hoped all would yet be well.

"Illness struck him before he

Continued on Page 12